Moving Beyond
Mediocrity

Moving Beyond Mediocrity

*Discovering principles that
will empower you to breakthrough*

John Andrews

New Wine Press

New Wine Ministries
PO Box 17
Chichester
West Sussex
United Kingdom
PO19 2AW

ISBN 978–1–903725–92–4

Typeset by CRB Associates, Reepham, Norfolk
Cover design by CCD, www.ccdgroup.co.uk
Printed in Malta

"John Andrews is becoming a prolific writer of good books. *Moving Beyond Mediocrity* tackles a real problem that affects many in society and even in the Christian Church: the lack of achievement and the ability to endure in the midst of trial. John's ability to use humour and his 'special stories' inspire the reader to meet the challenges of life."

Rev. Dr David E Carr
Senior Minister, Renewal Christian Centre
Solihull, UK

"John's new book is insightful, inspiring, interesting, illustrative and graced with humour. Truth is brought to light and applied with practical sharpness. An easy, enjoyable and mind-stretching read."

Rev. Paul C. Weaver
General Superintendent of the
Assemblies of God in Great Britain

"You'll laugh, you'll cry, and if you're wise you will heed the advice of a serious fellow traveller. Some say 'keep trucking'; Captain Kirk says, 'Beam me up, Scotty'; the Bible says, 'Blessed are those who have set their hearts on pilgrimage' (Psalm 84:5). John's book will inspire you, and then who will dare to imagine the destinations your journey will reveal!"

David Shearman
Senior Minister, Christian Centre
Nottingham, UK

Dedication

Grayson Jones
My Mach-busting mate

Over many years you have remained a faithful and
generous friend. As a leader you have demonstrated the
power of breakthrough and pioneered a path that others
have followed. I am richer for knowing you.
Thanks for everything.

*"A friend loves at all times,
    and a brother is born for adversity."*
(Proverbs 17:17)

Contents

Foreword

John Andrews is always worth reading, his unique insight and experience combine to make his books interesting and exciting.

It is refreshing to read someone who understands life so well. In this book you will not find any quick-fix solutions or a simple five-point plan to emerge from the challenges that life throws at us. Rather John has faced the issues of life with honesty and integrity that, put simply, is vitally needed in contemporary Christian literature. This book will have the combined effect of inspiring higher levels of faith whilst tempering concepts of how God works in our lives. Perhaps it is the latter of these that makes me enthusiastic about this book.

As a Christian leader, often the most frustrating part of my calling has been dealing with naïve and superficial expressions of Christian faith. At best, people who espouse these surface forms of faith are annoying but at worst they can damage both themselves and the reputation of God's people. Faith often entails processing "through the shakes" resulting in lasting expressions of God's goodness in communities around the world. It is the courage in the midst of fear that makes ordinary people extraordinary, simple people wise and weak people into heroes.

John is brilliantly positioned to write this book. He has proved God faithful and is an acknowledged leader. This is no light treatise on an unknown subject. It is the fruit of life experience as a husband, a father and a leader. He is now a well respected teacher engaged in the raising of a new generation of leaders. Years of active involvement in missions further adds to John's credibility.

Moving Beyond Mediocrity is a well written and timely book for those who want to live beyond the ordinary by daring to take up faith-filled adventure when God calls.

Paul Alexander
Principal
Mattersey Hall College and Graduate School

Preface

I had the privilege of being at the birth of all three of my children and in each case, in the midst of overwhelming joy, I confess I silently prayed, "Thank God I'm not a woman!" There's no doubt in my mind that if child-bearing had been entrusted to men the planet would never have to worry about the prospect of overcrowding.

As each of my children popped out into the world my concern was primarily for my wife, seeing the pain she endured. I never really considered the journey our babies made as they struggled to be born. A shrinking womb and violent contractions "encouraged" them through a narrow passage towards the wide open spaces of their new world. Once there, they would have room to grow, develop and explore ... but first they had to get out!

I once heard a leading gynaecologist say that if adults had to endure the same level of trauma that a baby experiences in the birth process, most of them would not survive. A baby's body is designed to contort, bend and stretch to enable a smooth passage as well as to endure the pressure. My son was born with bloodshot eyes and my youngest daughter was born with a pointy head ... simply due to the forcefulness of their birth journey.

Our experience as babies (thankfully we have no memory of this) gives us a clue to the profound life principle which is the underlying premise of this book. As we seek to move from one level of development to another, from a *small* place to a something bigger, from *containment* to expansion or from *average* to excellence, the journey necessary to accomplish this will almost certainly carry with it the "violence" of discomfort, the tremors of change and the challenge of living beyond the confines of our previous experience.

The writer to the Hebrews declares of Jesus:

> *"Although he was a son, he learned obedience from what he suffered and, once made perfect, he became the source of eternal salvation for all who obey him . . . "*
>
> (Hebrews 5:8–9)

Many want to achieve a standard of excellence cheaply and easily. They want glory without pain, recognition without rejection, prosperity without generosity and success with as few shakes as possible. However, as someone once said, "there are no short-cuts to anywhere that's worth going to". Though God's plans for us are hope-filled and glorious, the journey will not be without turbulence. The serious pilgrim needs to understand this truth and settle the issue within them once and for all. There's no free lunch. No gain without pain. No success in the Christian life without cost.

Success awaits those who face and conquer their fear. See you on the other side!

John Andrews
January 2007

Acknowledgements

All I've ever done would not have been possible without the love, encouragement, support and investment of other people. My wife, family and friends make me look much better than I am, and for this I am eternally grateful.

Dawn, I have no-one like you. During the writing of this book you faced and pressed through some immense personal challenges with unrelenting generosity. Your dignity and integrity, which I encountered both publicly and privately has only added to your beauty. I love you.

Elaina, Simeon and Beth-Anne – my biggest fans; I pray I'll always be a hero to you.

Dawn Andrews, Pippa Ankers, Julie Armstrong, Marilyn Gregory, Marion Hancock, Hannah Prosser and Marina Watts, my incredibly wonderful proof-readers, your generosity and support continue to amaze and humble me.

Paul Alexander, thank you for writing the foreword for this book. I am learning so much from your Mach-busting exploits. Thanks for your inspirational leadership and example.

Tim and all at New Wine Press, I appreciate you for believing in me enough to dare to publish anything I've written. Ta muchly.

Finally, my heavenly Father, if I were God the story of John Andrews would have been a short and miserable one, but thankfully You are You and I am me. My journal continues to fill with wonderful heaven-sent memories; Your grace convinces me there is much more. With all that I am I thank You.

Unnerved by the Unknown

"It was as smooth as a baby's bottom." This was how Captain Chuck Yeager[1] described the brave new world of Mach 1, a world beyond the sound barrier. However, none of this had seemed possible just a few days earlier. After three glide flights in his Bell X-1 rocket research aircraft, he had flown it to a speed of Mach 0.85 on his first powered flight on 29th August 1947. During his next six flights he encountered severe buffeting and sudden nose-up and nose-down trim changes. Then, on his eighth flight on 10th October, he lost pitch control altogether, as a shock wave formed along the hinge-line of the X-1's elevator. He reached Mach 0.997 that day but without pitch control it would have been foolish to continue. He was so close and yet so far away. Then on 14th October, he dropped away from the B-29 carrying his X-1, fired all four chambers of his engine in rapid sequence and bolted away from the launch aircraft. He shut down two of the chambers while testing the moveable tail on his plane. At 42,000 feet he reached Mach 0.92 and at this point relit a third chamber of his engine. The X-1 rapidly accelerated to Mach 0.98 and then, at 43,000 feet, the needle on his meter jumped off the scale. Captain Yeager had breached a barrier no human being had been through before.

As a sonic boom heralded a new technological age, Yeager went, quite literally, where no man had gone before, and was heralded as "The Fastest Man Alive!"[2]

Amazingly, within a generation, this achievement had paved the way for men to walk on the moon and even to sip champagne at Mach 2 on Concorde. Venturing into the unknown, Yeager and his peers had discovered a whole new world of possibilities, but in order to do it they had to press through the violence of the invisible sound barrier. To experience the fresh, smooth air of Mach 1 they had to break through and move beyond everything they had known.

As it is in the natural, so it is in the spiritual. God has new levels and new places He wants to take us but we must be prepared to press forward and break through the barriers that defy our progress. One of the things that stop us breaking through is the fact that we can become *unnerved by the unknown*. Not knowing what's out there is often enough to deter many from pressing through what I call the shakes – the anxiety caused by being asked by God to respond in faith when He asks us to do something we haven't done before.

This surely must have been how Mary felt, when faced with the angelic announcement. Luke introduces her to us.

Take a moment to read Luke 1:26–38.

Be careful, the story in this passage might be very familiar, but if we approach the Christmas story casually we are in danger of missing completely one of the greatest *Mach-busting* moments in the history of the world!

What it all boils down to is this, God was asking Mary to go where no person had gone before. No-one in human history had been asked to allow herself to become impregnated by God before, to carry His Son and become an extraordinary vessel in the redemptive purpose of heaven for the world. This was so far beyond Mary, that God might as well have asked her to break the speed of sound ... on foot! What He was asking of her was humanly impossible and socially inconceivable. God was asking Mary to break through to a new place, a higher level, somewhere beyond any limit thus far placed upon her. God could do it, but only if Mary agreed with Him!

Look at the beginning of the encounter again:

> "The angel went to her and said, 'Greetings, you who are highly favoured! The Lord is with you.' Mary was greatly troubled at his words and wondered what kind of greeting this might be."
>
> (Luke 1:28–29)

In the encounter that Mary had with the angel we see a number of shakes that potentially barred her way to success; the unexpected, something outside normal experience, it focused on potential and it would bring life-changing consequences.

► **It was unexpected**

A taxi passenger tapped his driver on the shoulder to ask him something. The driver screamed, lost control of the car, nearly hit a bus, went up on a pavement and stopped centimetres from a shop window. For a second everything went quiet in the cab then the driver spoke,

"Look mister, don't ever do that again. You scared the living daylights out of me!"

"I didn't realize that a little tap could scare you so much," the confused passenger apologised.

"Sorry, it's not really your fault," the driver replied. Today is my first day as a cab driver. I've been driving a hearse for the last twenty-five years."[3]

The day recorded in Luke 1, started as an ordinary day for Mary. She was going about her everyday business when she was confronted by an unexpected challenge from heaven.

Unexpectedness can be a huge barrier to breakthrough. It is one thing to be preparing for an event or a change but when something is thrust on us when we do not expect it, it can be enough to rock us back on our heels and stop us from even considering going forward. Our ability to handle the unexpected surprises of heaven and life determine whether we break through or buckle.

▶ *It was outside the range of her experience*
What the angel told Mary was outside the range of her experience, something for which she had no terms of reference. Her parents might well not believe her. She couldn't go to her computer and double click on the file marked, "Encounters with the angel Gabriel", or "What do I do when God asks to make you pregnant?" This was way off the chart and nothing could have prepared her for this challenge. Mary certainly had never experienced anything like it before and neither had anyone she knew.

When we're being asked to break through further in an area we've pioneered before, we have some experience and expertise to draw upon. But when God asks us to do something for which we have no information, no data, nothing to fall back on, that will always be a little scary.

God is always on the lookout for willing wombs! He's searching for people who are prepared to step forward into challenges, even when those challenges are above and beyond anything they have ever experienced before. He's looking for people like you. Mary was just an ordinary girl but she willingly made *womb for God* (sorry I couldn't resist that), and gave God the opportunity to do something breathtakingly extraordinary.

After our early morning prayer meeting, we usually have breakfast at a fast food outlet with golden arches. On one occasion I was about to place my order when the girl asked, "Are you having your usual?"

"Am I that predictable?" I thought.

Unfortunately, most of us are. We love routine and the comfort of the familiar. However, we must be careful not to allow this attitude to subtly militate against Mach-busting moments.

I challenge you to open yourself up to try new experiences even in the ordinary aspects of your life. If you love drinking tea, try coffee. If your favourite ice-cream is strawberry, try chocolate. If you have chips with everything, break out and try some pasta or rice (dare I suggest salad, or is that a step too far?)

Don't just stick to what you know, but rather train your life for new experiences by seeking them out and embracing them when they come. Moving to new levels and breaking through to life beyond the shakes will inevitably involve experiences, opportunities and demands beyond the normal routine of what has gone before. We must come to accept that breakthrough by its very definition will take us to places we have never been before and for which we have no terms of reference.

▶ **It focused on potential not actuality**

> *"How will this be . . . since I am a virgin?"*
>
> (Luke 1:34)

As a woman, Mary had the potential to become pregnant but as yet this was untried potential. It is one thing possessing the potential to get pregnant . . . it is another thing entirely actually to become pregnant. When God approached Mary, He was seeking to move her from potential to actuality.

The dictionary describes potential as, "That which may or might but does not now act or exist ... latent ... expressing possibility".[4]

Someone once said, "Life is like a fifteen-speed bike. Most of us have gears we never use."

How true that is! Many people love the concept of potential without taking any steps to realize it. One of the things I've discovered is the danger and allure of the potential trap. "He's got potential ... She could be something..." It sounds wonderful (and it is) but at some stage that which is latent needs to come to life and that which *may* or *might* needs to *be*! Many live a life of unrealized potential. They never actually do anything but are comforted by the fact that the potential is there.

> "My mother said to me, 'If you become a soldier, you'll be a general; if you become a monk, you'll end up as a Pope.' Instead I became a painter and wound up as Picasso."
>
> (Pablo Picasso, 1881–1973)

What potential has God already placed inside you? What latent talent is resident in you from the moment of your conception?

When God takes us to the brink of breakthrough He confronts us with our own potential and encourages us to actually do that which is within us to do. God wasn't asking Mary to do anything that she did not have the potential to do. Genetically, physically, it was all there ... she just needed to make a decision to allow it to happen and with God's magnificent help realize that which was within her.

Everything God asks of *us* is already possible because of the incredible partnership of His power and our ability. As we do what we can, He does what He can ... and the result is breakthrough. Mary couldn't get pregnant alone and God couldn't become flesh without a womb. *In partnership, Mary's potential was realized and God's power was released!*

▶ **It carried consequences**

Apparently, life is getting riskier ... or is it just that the health and safety police are getting more zealous?

According to a report compiled by the Home and Leisure Accident Surveillance System:

- 37 people hurt themselves using teapot warmers in 1999, compared to 20 in 1998.
- Trouser injuries jumped, rising from 5,137 to 5,945 (one woman ironed hers while still wearing them).
- Hospital cases caused by socks and tights injuries rose by nearly 1,000 to 10,773.
- 3,421 were hurt by clothes baskets, 146 by bread bins, and 329 by toilet roll holders.
- Bin-bag injuries climbed from 957 to 1,317 making them four times as dangerous as meat cleavers.
- Mishaps with birdbaths rose from 117 to 311.

There is some good news. Injuries inflicted by armchairs fell from 18,690 to 16,662.[5]

If there are dangers and potentially painful consequences to such nondescript things as those listed above, then don't you think the risks attached to breakthrough might perhaps increase just a little? Even though God is in control, even though He will perfect His purpose for us, *this side* of breakthrough the risks can seem daunting.

Mary's risks were massive on at least three levels:

1. *Physically,* she was literally putting her body on the line, willingly embracing all the demands and dangers carrying and delivering a baby would entail.

2. *Relationally*, she was putting her future with Joseph on the line. The Bible makes it clear that he was a good, upright and honourable man, but even his resolve would be tested by Mary's condition and the apparent cause. Can you imagine, "Joseph darling I'm pregnant, but an angel told me I'm carrying God's son"?

3. *Socially*, Mary, a young girl from Nazareth, was risking it all. If it was discovered she was pregnant out of wedlock, at best she was looking at divorce and disgrace, at worst a painful death by stoning. Not great options for a teenager.

This was no walk in the park. There would be consequences for Mary acting on God's word, and in order to break through she had to face the price tag honestly and make a decision based on facts, not on some fanciful whim. Faith does not ignore facts . . . it faces them. Faith doesn't run from the price tag, it knows exactly how much it is going to cost . . . but still decides to pay. As one wag once said:

"Don't be afraid to go out on a limb . . . that's where the fruit is."

Mary's Mach-busting moment is recorded for us:

"I am the Lord's servant . . . May it be to me as you have said."
(Luke 1:38)

This was her defining moment, when a girl from Nazareth became the unsung heroine of the redemption story. This was the moment when the angels applauded, when God stood up from His throne and when hell and all its hordes trembled. She trusted God's words spoken by an angel and engaged with heaven in a way that today elevates her, in my humble opinion, to the position of being the greatest (certainly the most blessed) woman that ever lived. She experienced a world in God, which was only possible because she was prepared to go where she had to go, got through the barriers before her and pressed on regardless of the cost. This was not easy. It cost her in every way, but the rewards to her and the world are beyond calculation. God asked Mary for her womb and despite not knowing what lay beyond the request she generously gave it.

What is God asking of you and what is stopping you from giving?

"I don't know what will happen if I give more, go on that mission trip, serve my neighbour, give up my job, go to Bible School or serve my church."

I don't know what will happen either, but what I can tell you is this, every time He's asked me to give something away, He's never once let me down. Whatever He has asked of me hasn't always been what I wanted or expected ... but it has always been worth it.

If we are going to break through and, like Mary experience a Mach-busting moment, we must learn to conquer our nervousness over the unknown. We must learn to trust God despite being asked to journey to a world beyond our experience. Only then can we hope to enjoy success beyond the shakes.

Notes _____

1. Now General Yeager.
2. www.chuckyeager.com – his official web-site.
3. John, J. and Stibbe, M., *A Bucket of Surprises* (Monarch, 2002), p. 196.
4. *Oxford Dictionary.*
5. John, J. and Stibbe, M., "A 2001 report" in *A Barrel of Fun* (Monarch, 2003), p. 54.

No Gain without Pain

"Great God this is an awful place!"

English explorer Captain Robert Falcon Scott had good reason to be unimpressed by the South Pole because when he arrived there on 17th January 1912 he discovered a Norwegian flag already marking the spot. It had been left there by Roald Amundsen on 14th December 1911, together with a note asking Scott to report Amundsen's triumph to the King of Norway.

Disappointment dogged every step of the return for Scott's party. It was a journey legendary for the selflessness of Captain Oates, whose frostbitten feet were hindering the progress of the team. Oates left the tent during a blizzard with the words, "I may be some time." He was never seen again, perishing in the frozen wasteland. Tragically, despite Oates' heroism, none of the party survived, but before Scott died he found time to write their epitaph:

> "Had we lived, I should have had a tale to tell of the hardihood, endurance and courage of my companions ... These rough notes and our dead bodies must tell the tale."[1]

If we want to live a life of gain we must first break through the pain barriers that often attempt to hem us in. We must settle this fact right at the beginning of any great venture of faith. Whatever the venture might be, there will never be any gain without breaking through a barrier of pain.

> "Do not pray for easy lives. Pray to be stronger men. Do not pray for tasks equal to your powers; pray for powers equal to your tasks." [2]

Many want to live on the other side of success and enjoy the pleasure it brings, but we must understand that in order to enjoy what is beyond the line, we must first cross it. If we cannot get through the pain barriers around or within us, then we will struggle to enjoy the freedom that lies beyond the boundary and we will rarely experience Mach-busting moments. Pain attempts to keep us boxed in, but we must do all in our power to break out and experience the "more" which God has destined for us.

Take a moment to read 2 Corinthians 6:3–13.

The Apostle Paul knew something about crossing the pain barrier. It is too easy to be intoxicated by the glory of Paul's numerous and monumental achievements while missing the considerable personal cost. It is convenient and comforting if our theology permits us the luxury of celebrating his success while excluding his pain from the final reckoning. Paul's inspirational example demonstrates to us that we can gain success beyond the shakes of pain.

The pain of pain

> *"Rather, as servants of God we commend ourselves in every way: in great endurance; in troubles, hardships and distresses."*
>
> (2 Corinthians 6:4)

The words that Paul uses here, in their original form point not only to severe pressure but to the idea of restraint. The word "distresses" for example, can literally be translated "narrowness of a room or place". It gives the sense of the idea of the constraint of a siege. These aren't just passing issues, Paul is referring to things that are pressing in on him with such ferocity that it feels like he is under siege, leaving him feeling hemmed in and restricted. Paul is contending, not just with momentary or fleeting pain, but with pain that is attempting to take up residence in his life.

Thus we see the tyrannous power of pain. Its merciless quest is to enslave and control its victims, condemning them to the prison cell of self-pity, regret, fear and blame. Its plan is always to reduce not enlarge, to restrict without prospect of release, eradicating any inspiration through intimidation.

In this passage Paul outlines significant pain barriers he has had to work through and gain the ascendancy over. Perhaps you'll recognise some of them:

▶ *The pain of opposition*

> "... in beatings, imprisonments and riots; in hard work, sleepless nights and hunger."
>
> (2 Corinthians 6:5)

Paul outlines some of the opposition he endured from those both within and without the Church. This is graphically illustrated later in the same letter, when in 2 Corinthians 11:23–29 we are given brutal details of Paul's experiences in the cause of the gospel:

> "I have laboured and toiled and have often gone without sleep; I have known hunger and thirst and have often gone without food; I have been cold and naked."
>
> (2 Corinthians 11:27)

Okay, who wants to join?

The pain of opposition can be, for many of us, a step too far. Once it begins to get rough and people start to give us a hard time we want out. When opposition kicks in, the exit door looms large and lures us with the attractive option of taking the path of least resistance. However, if we leave through this door, not only will the success we crave elude us but tragically, we'll also take our pain with us.

▶ *The pain of being misunderstood*

> *". . . through glory and dishonour, bad report and good report; genuine, yet regarded as impostors; known, yet regarded as unknown . . ."*
>
> (2 Corinthians 6:8–9)

Imagine being misunderstood by the very people you have poured your life into. The idea behind the use of the word *unknown* is one of being ignored, rejected, not recognised for one's credentials. Jesus knew this pain:

> *"He was in the world, and though the world was made through him, the world did not recognise him. He came to that which was his own, but his own did not receive him."*
>
> (John 1:10–11)

This is not nice. In fact, if you've experienced this, it's pretty horrible! This can be one of the most painful pain barriers we ever have to break through, when people, especially people we love and have invested ourselves into, misunderstand our lives, our message and our heart.

▶ *The pain of disappointment*

> *"We are not withholding our affection from you, but you are withholding yours from us."*
>
> (2 Corinthians 6:12)

Disappointment can be a painful thing. It may be the result of personal failure, other people letting us down or dislocated expectations . . . things you had hoped for but that have not, for whatever reason, materialised:

> "*. . . Demas, because he loved this world, has deserted me . . .* "
>
> (2 Timothy 4:10)

These are among some of the last recorded words of Paul and although the whole passage is upbeat and powerfully positive, Paul cannot disguise his deep and painful disappointment at the desertion of one of his dearest friends.

If we are going to live in success beyond the shakes, then we must get through the pain of disappointment. If we don't manage to do this, the place that should have been a record of our triumph will become our grave.

Okay, enough of the pain already. How did Paul get through such pain and move to the other side of the shakes? What lessons can we learn in the twenty-first century from this first-century Mach-busting giant?

In this passage Paul gives us some principles he has proved in pain busting situations:

▶ *Focus on the right stuff*

> "*. . . dying, and yet we live on; beaten, and yet not killed.*"
>
> (2 Corinthians 6:9)

Paul had a choice to make: put simply, to focus on the dying or the living, to fix his eyes on the beating or the fact that he was still alive!

I remember one occasion when my youngest daughter Beth-Anne cut her finger. It was only a tiny little cut, but for a three year old there was blood and when there's blood, it's serious! So Mummy kindly and tenderly put a plaster over the cut. For an hour or so, Beth-Anne walked around with her "poorly finger" in the air for everyone to see, in the hope of some sympathy. However, as the day wore on she forgot all about her finger until, that is, I asked, "Is your finger better now?" Instantly she shot her plastered finger straight up into the air and with a face that would have melted the hardest heart said, "Oh no Daddy, it's still sore!"

Aren't we all a little bit like this? We experience some pain and if we're not careful we enjoy wearing it like a plaster for the whole world to see, so that everyone can sympathise with us. The pain remains close to the surface, quickly introduced to any and every conversation, subtly dominating our agenda.

We need to understand that our focus is crucial. Try something for me. It's not new or original, but humour me anyway. Put your thumb up about twelve inches in front of your face. Now, focus completely on your thumb. What happens to the background? If you're doing it right, the background should be out of focus. Now, focus completely on the background. What happens to your thumb? If you're doing it right, your thumb should be out of focus.

The lesson is profoundly simple. If we concentrate on the pain the rest of our life, including all the good bits, will blur out of focus. Conversely, if we choose to concentrate on the good things, principles of life and truth, then the pain will blur out of focus even if it doesn't completely disappear. Paul teaches us that what we focus on is our choice. We decide what we look at. Paul chose to focus on life not death and instructs us that we can do the same, *if we want to*.

What has your focus?

Are you focusing on the dying or the living?

► **Speak the right words**

"sorrowful, yet always rejoicing . . . "

(2 Corinthians 6:10)

Paul was able to get through pain barriers of disappointment and misunderstanding because *he made a choice to rejoice:*

"Rejoice in the Lord always. I will say it again: Rejoice!"

(Philippians 4:4)

Paul didn't write these words from the penthouse suite of the Hilton Hotel, he wrote them from a prison cell. He learned to rejoice in the toughest situations of life, as Acts 16:25 powerfully illustrates.

Solomon teaches us that the power of life and death is in the tongue (Proverbs 18:21). However, it is important to see this statement in the light of the previous verse in which he concludes:

"From the fruit of his mouth a man's stomach is filled;
with the harvest from his lips he is satisfied."

From this we can see that not only does the confession of our lips to some extent *reflect* the condition our soul, but also that our confession *feeds* our soul! In other words, our words are not only *fruit* (expressing the heart), but *food* (feeding the heart). For this reason we need to work on our confession when the pain comes. It is important to remember that even in the pain, God is still good and He remains awesome in every way. When we hit the pain barriers of life and purpose, our confession becomes vitally important in feeding and sustaining our soul. If we confess the pain, the wounds and the misery, then these things become the staple diet of our lives, for what we speak out, we inevitably take in! Conversely, if we confess the works of God over our lives, what delicious, life-giving food this is for the soul.

What words are in your mouth?

What confession is forming the diet for your soul?

► *Do the right things*

> *"... poor, yet making many rich ... "*

(2 Corinthians 6:10)

Paul decided to keep doing the things that he knew were the right things to do: giving, loving, serving and sharing. In another portion of the same letter he writes:

> *"So I will very gladly spend for you everything I have and expend myself as well."*

(2 Corinthians 12:15)

Whatever *the Corinthians'* decision, Paul had already made *his*!

That's the mark of greatness; to press through and continue doing the right things, even when all we want to do is withdraw into self-pity and defeat. It is all too tempting to sacrifice our commitment to doing what we know is the right thing to do, because of the pain we are experiencing. In moments of pain, when it comes to doing the right thing, the best form of defence is attack!

A close friend of mine, in the cause of serving Jesus, encountered some challenging pain barriers. Through no fault of her own, her friendship and some personal confidences were betrayed by someone she loved and trusted. The knowledge of this was like having a sword plunged into her heart. It would have been the easiest thing in the world for her to walk away, give up and use her pain as an excuse never to do the right thing again. But that's not what she did. Instead she decided to fight back, not by seeking to defend her reputation, or by demanding vengeance but by serving, giving and loving. She continued to do the things she believed in. Over a number of months, I saw her serve through tears, give to others though in need herself, maintain a dignified silence when given the opportunity to gossip and consistently make choices to do the right things. As she did so, she broke through intimidating obstacles, modelling a life of dignity, strength and character. Though "poor", she made others rich. Her decision to do the right things regardless, was and continues to be an inspiration to me. To respect and honour such a woman is no hard thing – thank you!

What's your excuse for not doing the right thing?

"He said this . . . "

"She said that . . . "

"He did . . . "

"She didn't"!

"Why should I continue to do the right thing in the face of such pain?"

The answer is simple, but you might not like it. The reason we need to choose to do the right thing, is because *it's the right thing.* Even if no-one benefits from these choices (although doing the right thing will always bless somebody), we can encourage ourselves with the knowledge that we refused to become another victim of pain, and were empowered instead to breathe the pure Mach-busting, unpolluted air of freedom.

▶ **Build on the right values**

> " . . . *having nothing, and yet possessing everything."*
>
> (2 Corinthians 6:10)

What a statement, what a hope, what a philosophy! One of the great keys to living in the power of breakthrough, is to understand who you are and what you have; to view your life and its wealth, not as the world sees it, but as God sees it. Even in the midst of difficulty and material impoverishment, Paul knew that he was still one of the richest men on planet earth because he understood that his riches lay, not in stuff, or fading glory but in eternal truth, eternal treasure and eternal investment.

If we know we possess everything, then "having nothing" will be of little consequence to us. If we build our lives on eternal values, then we will rarely be seduced or disappointed by earthly, temporal shortcomings, by things that glitter but turn out to be plastic! If our lives are built on solid rock then we need not fear the storm as its probing rain searches out the sand. Paul said:

> *"So we fix our eyes not on what is seen, but on what is unseen. For what is seen is temporary, but what is unseen is eternal."*
>
> (2 Corinthians 4:18)

If our lives are built on the wrong values, pain will always, ultimately, get the better of us. If we refuse to be enticed off the bedrock of eternal truths, however, then no weapon formed against us will prosper and although not immune from pain, we will not be mastered by it.

My father is a fantastic man. He is not only one of my dearest friends, but he ranks as one of my heroes and this story will perhaps illustrate why. Just before he was due to retire it was discovered he was suffering from angina. As a result he was offered medical redundancy, before which his company required a medical examination. During the medical my father was asked a question which he in all innocence answered honestly. However, this answer was turned against him to the extent that it threatened his promised redundancy. When the word got out, his work colleagues "encouraged" him to lie in order to get the money. My father's response was magnificent.

"If I lie to get the money, then everything I have stood for as a Christian in this place will be lost. I will be remembered as the Christian who lied for his redundancy. I would rather leave with my testimony intact than with the money."

Building on Kingdom values cost my father a lot of money but as he told me after the event, "I haven't missed it and I'm more blessed than I've ever been." When the pain of short-term loss threatened, Alex Andrews, my wonderful father, reminded himself that he already possessed everything!

What values are you building on?

There is success beyond the shakes but we'll never get there unless we are prepared to press through some significant pain barriers and push on into victory. These truly are Mach-busting moments, violent, difficult and intimidating, but to get beyond them is life itself. Don't let the shakes put you off – press on to the freedom of success!

Notes _____

1. Harrison, Ian (compiler), *The Book of Firsts* (Cassell Illustrated, 2003), p. 16.
2. Quote by Phillips Brooks in David Shibley, *Heaven's Heroes* (New Leaf, 1994), p. 133.

The Fear Factor

The first person to cross the Niagara River on a tightrope was Frenchman Jean François Gravelet, better known as Charles Blondin. He achieved this in 1859, an accomplishment described by the *New York Times* as "the greatest feat of the nineteenth century". He crossed the river on a manila rope only 75mm thick, spanning the gorge about a mile downstream from the falls themselves. He subsequently made the crossing blindfolded, performed handstands and somersaults on the rope, pushed a wheelbarrow across it twice and twice made the crossing while carrying his manager, Harry Colcord, on his back. He even cooked an omelette midway across and lowered it on a rope to passengers on the tourist boat *Maid of the Mist*, who were watching from the river below!

Others undoubtedly inspired by Blondin's "heroics" included Annie Edson Taylor, who in 1901 had herself sealed in a padded barrel (emphasis on the word padded?) and became the first person to survive a *plunge* over the falls. Afterwards, she advised no-one to copy her and indeed it was another ten years before someone attempted to repeat the feat. At the time of her amazing stunt, Annie Taylor told the press she was forty-three years old, she was in fact sixty-three.

It should be said that not everyone was successful in their attempts to beat the falls. In 1901 for example, Maud Willard (USA), died while taking her dog with her in a barrel through the rapids. It seems that her dog, in a panic, unfortunately pressed its nose against the air vent, and inadvertently suffocated its hapless owner.[1] Who said a dog was man's best friend?

To face and conquer the awesome might of the Niagara Falls, one has to be able to face and overcome fear. Blondin, Taylor and all the others who attempted to tame the falls had to wrestle with the fear of failure, injury or even death, in order to achieve their goals. If they were going to enjoy the glory of the calm waters, they had to endure the fear-filled, violent turbulence of the falls. Rather them than me!

Take a moment to read Joshua 1:1–11.

Joshua was facing a Niagara Falls-sized challenge. Ironically, he had been there before and knew exactly what it would entail, but this was the biggest test of his life as a man and a leader. God was calling him not only to cross the border of a country, but also to break through the boundary of fear. To do the latter would be a key to ensuring success in the former.

Though the passage does not explicitly state that Joshua was afraid, it is nonetheless striking that in the space of four verses God says virtually the same thing to Joshua three times:

► *As a leader*

> *"Be strong and courageous, because you will lead these people to inherit the land I swore to their forefathers to give them."*

> (Joshua 1:6)

► *As a law keeper*

> *"Be strong and very courageous. Be careful to obey all the law my servant Moses gave you; do not turn from it to the right or to the left,*

that you may be successful wherever you go. Do not let this Book of the Law depart from your mouth; meditate on it day and night, so that you may be careful to do everything written in it. Then you will be prosperous and successful."

(Joshua 1:7–8)

► **As a learner**

"Have I not commanded you? Be strong and courageous. Do not be terrified; do not be discouraged, for the LORD your God will be with you wherever you go."

(Joshua 1:9)

Joshua was a seasoned soldier and a man of God, trained under one of the greatest leaders that ever lived. He had seen it all and done most of it, so why would God have to tell him three times to be strong and courageous . . . to not be afraid? Perhaps it was because the great man was afraid! God doesn't waste words; He says only what He has to say. God speaks to the heart of this outstanding man on the eve of this historic campaign and encourages him to cross the fear line . . . to face up to the fear and take on the challenge before him.

"Fear is the darkroom where Satan develops your negatives."[2]

But why might Joshua have been afraid?

Fear of past memories

Joshua had been here before. He had been one of the twelve, commissioned and sent out by Moses to spy out the land (Numbers 13:1–33). He had witnessed the glory of the promise first hand and the devastating disappointment of having it snatched from his grasp. He had to endure forty years of aimless

wandering in the purposeless wilderness, when all the time, he
and his friend Caleb had seen, tasted and enjoyed the land. As
the line of one song put it, "If I didn't see such riches, I could
live with being poor."

The fear created by past memories can be a powerful
deterrent as we seek to move forward into the future God has
for us. What has happened to us, around us or even because of
us, can restrict us from moving forward.

> *"Brothers, I do not consider myself yet to have taken hold of it. But
> one thing I do:* **Forgetting what is behind** *and* **straining towards
> what is ahead,** *I* **press on** *toward the goal to win the prize for which
> God has called me heavenward in Christ Jesus."*
>
> (Philippians 3:13–14, emphasis added)

The word *strain*, points to the idea of someone stretching
themselves out towards something. It's the image of a runner
leaning forward as he reaches out for the finishing line.
Everything is put into the straining process, with every muscle
and sinew and every ounce of energy directed into it.

It is interesting that in the above verse Paul says, *". . . one
thing I do . . . "* yet as we look at the verse he's actually doing *two
things*, namely, *"forgetting what is behind"* and *"straining towards
what is ahead"*. Is this a contradiction? I think not, for in Paul's
thinking the two things are in fact one thing. In effect he teaches
us, *we cannot move forward if we refuse to forget what is behind.*
Letting go of the past is a prerequisite to taking hold of our
future.

God used similar language when speaking to Israel in Isaiah
43:16–19. He reminds them of what He did in their past, *"he
who made a way through the sea, a path through the mighty waters"*
(v. 16) and then He says, *"Forget the former things; do not dwell on
the past"* (v. 18).

But why? The answer is clear:

> *"See, I am doing a new thing!*
> *Now it springs up; do you not perceive it?*
> *I am making a way in the desert*
> *and streams in the wasteland."*

(Isaiah 43:19)

Had the people continued to dwell on the past, they would have certainly missed the "new thing" that God was about to do. In the past He made a dry place where there was sea, but in the future He would make a stream where once only desert had been! In more ways than one He was literally doing a new thing.

I knew a young leader who after a courageous attempt to lead his first church, through circumstances partly outside of his control, decided to resign his position. Though he had achieved a good measure of success, he nonetheless believed that he had failed. Within a few months of leaving his first church, however, he was invited to consider leading another church. Although he believed this was the will of God for him, fear threatened to enslave his heart. As he prayed, the memories of his past "failure" haunted him and caused him to privately hesitate over the new opportunity before him. He faced a choice, to hold on to the past and allow its fear to cast a dark shadow over his future, or to decide to stop looking back and deliberately look forward, facing his fears by turning his back on them! Today, that young man leads so well and inspires so many to live for Jesus that few would ever guess or imagine that because of the fear of past failure he almost gave up on his call to lead. Thank God he didn't.

We need to quit the dangerous looking back habit today and train ourselves to "strain" forward. Looking back at the wrong things, for the wrong reasons will always cause us to miss our present and seriously jeopardize our future.

Fear of present mantle

Joshua was taking over from Moses. You know, the highly intelligent well educated man, who took on Pharaoh, the most powerful man in the world at that time, and with nothing more than the promise of God and a stick ... won! The same Moses who led over two million people across the Red Sea, went up the mountain and came down with the Law ... not to mention a shiny face radiating from the glory of God. The one who supervised the design and building of the Tabernacle ... yes him! The people had just mourned the great man for thirty days and now all eyes are on Joshua.

Was God hinting at Joshua's fear of taking Moses' mantle when He stated, *"Moses my servant is dead"* (Joshua 1:2)?

Whether He was or not, I'm glad God did not leave Joshua with a fact that stated the obvious. Instead God added two glorious words, *"Now then ... "*

He didn't say, "Now then, try and fill Moses' sandals if you can and see how you get on," or "Now then, I'm not sure if you'll ever be a Moses, but let's see how you do," or "Now then, there's no way you'll ever match up to Moses, but I'll be with you anyway."

God says:

> *"**Now then, you** and all these people, get ready to cross the Jordan River into the land I am about to give them – to the Israelites."*
>
> (Joshua 1:2, emphasis added)

It is striking that God takes the time to specifically speak to Joshua:

" . . . you and all these people . . . "

(Joshua 1:2, emphasis added)

I will give you every place where you set your foot . . . "

(Joshua 1:3)

*"As I was with Moses, **so I will be with you**; I will never leave you nor forsake you."*

(Joshua 1:5, emphasis added)

God is not just speaking to the people, He's speaking directly to Joshua. He's not just talking about purpose, He's addressing a person!

David was a big lad. A former coal-miner from Yorkshire, he was the sort of man you would want on your side if a fight broke out. Yet he was terrified of flying. The problem was this fear was getting in the way of him going on a global mission trip. There was no other option of getting there except by plane. David had a choice to either allow the fear of falling out of the sky in a metal box with only a life-jacket for protection stop him from enjoying an experience of a life-time, or to face his fears, get on the plane and get to the other side ... the destination, not heaven that is! With lots of encouragement from his friends, and it must be said, the occasional sleeping tablet, David pressed through the shakes of fear and "enjoyed" the clear blue skies of success.

If God asks you to carry a mantle – it's because *you* can!

If you wear size nine shoes He won't ask you to fill size eleven!

If you're called Joshua He won't accidentally call you Moses!

If He asks you to do it, it's because He wants *you* to do it!

Don't fear the challenge of whatever mantle God is asking you to accept, rather fear the mediocrity of never being all you can be. That's a greater terror which we must overcome.

Fear of future mandate

Joshua looked across that relatively small river and saw the land of promise. He knew this was God's heart and plan and he also knew he was the man God had chosen to lead the people over.

Could it be that the challenge of this future mandate weighed heavy on this new leader?

I would be surprised if it wasn't doing so. Joshua knew what was required. He understood people would die and suffer in the campaigns that lay ahead. He was aware that the nation would be tested to the very edge of its endurance. He knew he and his family would be put under the most incredible pressure and that giants waited for them behind walled cities. His was the mandate to lead a people to victory and then to help them rule in peace. A lot rested on the shoulders of Joshua, son of Nun.

It's 1996, the quarter-final of soccer's European Championship, and England and Spain are deadlocked at the end of extra time . . . the match has gone to penalties. Standing over the ball for England, about to take his penalty, is a young man called Stuart Pearce. The eyes of everyone in Wembley stadium and most of the nation are on him, hopes and dreams wrapped up in the next few seconds of time. So what, I hear you say (especially the non-soccer fans)! Rewind to six years earlier in another penalty shoot-out, when the same young man had stood over the ball in the semi-final of the soccer World Cup, against arch-rivals Germany. Both teams were neck and neck, the tension was tangible. Pearce stepped up, blasted the ball towards the goal, only to see it saved by the German goalkeeper. England lost and Germany went on to win the trophy. Now fast-forward to 1996. Most footballers would have abdicated their responsibility that day, run a mile from the prospect of missing yet another crucial penalty for England . . . but not Pearce. He stepped up and with passionate zeal, hammered the ball into the back of the net. His reaction afterwards was in marked contrast to his uncontrollable tears six years before. He punched the air, screamed at the crowd and roared his delight in a way that would have made the three lions on his chest proud. Imagine for a moment (even if you don't like football), the fear he must have had inside him, as he walked from the centre circle to take the penalty. The future beckoned . . . and only fear stood in the way.

Everything God asks of us will probably be a little scary. Mach-busting moments are like that. Fear is natural and dare I say it, normal. That's why God spends so much time helping us to address it . . . because it happens a lot! The most courageous acts I've ever seen have been performed when fear loomed large and roared with intent, when the easiest thing would have been to walk away, abdicate responsibility and quit. God wants to take us to places and get us to do things, ordained by Him, for His glory, which this side of the line, will always be somewhat frightening. Sometimes the pressure of the mandate, the challenge of tomorrow can intimidate us to draw back and refuse to take the kick!

I love the Mach-busting record of Joshua's words and actions after this dialogue with God. Having heard God's promises and received the assurances. Joshua has faced up to fear and decided to cross over anyway:

> *"So Joshua ordered the officers of the people: 'Go through the camp and tell the people, "Get your supplies ready. Three days from now you will cross the Jordan here to go in and take possession of the land the LORD your God is giving you for your own."'"*

(Joshua 1:10–11)

Fear stands like a foreboding bully trying to stop us from moving forward. It will use the past, present or future to intimidate and deter us. But Joshua, in a magnificent Mach-busting episode, teaches us that fear can be faced up to and conquered. If we are willing to press through the shakes of fear, success awaits us beyond the river, just as it did for Joshua.

> "Proper courage is wise courage. It's acting wisely, acting wisely when fear would have a man act otherwise. It is the endurance of the soul in spite of fear – wisely."[3]

Notes

1. *Book of Firsts*, op. cit., pp. 28–29.
2. John, J. and Stibbe, M., *A Box of Delights* (Monarch, 2001), p. 67.
3. O'Brien, T., *If I Die in a Combat Zone* (Harper Perennial, first published 1973), p. 137.

Crossing the Cost Line

The English Channel, linking the Atlantic Ocean with the North Sea and separating England from the mainland of Europe, is one of the world's busiest shipping lanes. Despite the traffic and the treacherous currents, swimmers still brave the waters to emulate a feat first achieved by Englishman Matthew Webb. On 24th August 1875 the twenty-seven-year-old merchant navy captain, covered in a layer of porpoise grease for insulation against the cold water, stepped into the sea close to Admiralty Pier in Dover, England. He swam continuously until twenty-one hours forty-five minutes later he emerged from the water at Cap Griz Nez in France and became the first person to swim the English Channel.

By the time New Yorker Gertrude Ederle became the first woman to swim the Channel on 6th August 1926, fifty-one years later, only four men had repeated Webb's feat. Gertrude had overcome the disappointment of failing to swim the Channel a year earlier, being pulled out of the water just seven miles from the finish. "People said women couldn't swim the Channel, but I proved they could."

Other achievements in the Channel worthy of note are:

- In 1961 Antonio Albertondo made the first double crossing
- In 1981 Jon Erikson became the first person to swim the Channel three times England–France–England–France
- In 1988 Richard Davey set a record for the fastest France–England swim – eight hours five minutes
- In 1994 Chad Hundeby set a record for the fastest England–France swim – seven hours seventeen minutes.[1]

One has to marvel at the sacrifice and cost involved in simply achieving such a goal. The training, the pain, the cold and the endless lonely hours in the water, all reflect the major cost paid in order to achieve the goal.

No dream can ever be fulfilled; no venture will ever be accomplished without having to cross the cost line ... not just once, but on numerous occasions. To imagine that anything of significance can be achieved without cost or sacrifice is naïve at best and foolishness at worst. Anything of value, anything worth having, keeping and living for will cost us. In fact, it must cost us. Without cost there is usually no value and without a sense of value, that which is precious gets treated with lazy contempt. Great marriages, businesses, churches and dreams cost ... and if they don't, they'll never be anything more than mediocre!

Take a moment to read Genesis 29:14–30.

When confronted with a formidable cost line, with the violent shakes of the price-tag, it is crucial we learn to think the right way about what lies before us. Wrong thinking will inflate the price beyond the bounds of affordability. It will always be beyond our reach. However, right thinking can empower us to pay whatever is needed to achieve that which God has put in our hearts. Rachel was "expensive" but Jacob didn't seem to mind paying ... I wonder why?

Anything of worth will always cost

"I'll work for you seven years in return for your younger daughter Rachel."

(Genesis 29:18)

Jacob understood a simple principle: in order to attain anything of value, it's going to cost. He did not want, or expect to get Rachel on the cheap. For a woman of such beauty so highly prized by her father, he knew the price tag would be high and accepted that he would have to pay it.

The freebie culture that so many are familiar with starts with a mentality that hopes we can get things of value on the cheap. Now, don't get me wrong, there is nothing wrong with getting a bargain or asking for one, but this is not what I am talking about. I'm speaking of those who have factored cost out of the equation of their life *entirely*. They want good grades without study, good jobs without working, good marriages without investing and great blessing without contributing. They believe that God, the world and everything in it owes them and if they can get away without paying, they will. This is a cheap and nasty mentality and it will only ever produce a cheap and nasty life. Bargain hunting is one thing, but free-loading is something else entirely. If you expect to pay for things of value, then it won't be a shock to you. Then, if you do get a bargain, you'll enjoy it as a "cream on the cake" blessing.

What greatness are you demanding of your life?

Greatness will cost! If we settle for smallness and mediocrity it will cost us virtually nothing, although in the end such actions will be extremely expensive. Average costs nothing. We don't even have to try to be average, but greatness ain't cheap. If we want a Mach-busting moment, to press through the barriers and get to the other side, at some point you and I are going to have to pay.

Jacob was asked to work and wait seven years for the woman he loved.

Such a fact begs the questions, how much are you prepared to pay and how patient are you prepared to be for the thing you believe in?

"I want it, and I want it now!" I'm a little tired of the attitude that life is like an ATM. Just insert the card, enter the request and we get what we ask for, immediately! Life doesn't tend to work like that, and neither does God!

Too many are ready to give up on their dreams, their marriage, their job, even their church because they are not quite getting what they hoped as quickly as they planned. The questions remain:

- Is it worth working for?
- Is it worth fighting for?
- Is it worth waiting for?

Jacob wanted Rachel so badly that he was willing to work and wait.

If we're not prepared to work and wait for something, then that reveals it is worth little to us. It is impossible to ignore the cost line when handling anything of value. Don't be cheap. Go all the way for the things you believe in and cross the cost line.

The *cause* must always be greater than the *cost*

> "So Jacob served seven years to get Rachel, but they seemed like only a few days to him because of his love for her."

(Genesis 29:20)

These must be among the most romantic words in the whole of the Bible. Years seemed like days to Jacob, simply because he wasn't looking at the cost; rather he had his eyes on the *cause* . . . Rachel!

We will never be prepared to pay whatever is asked of us, unless we are convinced that it is worth it. Life teaches that when the cause is deemed greater than the cost:

- A husband will say no to adultery when he had the opportunity to say yes
- A mother will work extra so her daughter can have those dance lessons
- An athlete will get up at 5:00 a.m. every morning to train
- A teacher will stay at school a little bit longer and give a little bit more, without pay, simply for the love of the children he or she teaches
- Young men will even strap explosives to their chest and pull the trigger

We are faced with the *cause/cost* tension virtually every day of our lives. We dream, believe and hope but each day we are challenged as to our preparedness to pay the cost for what we claim to actually believe in. Whether the cost means change, money, time or effort it will always be an attainable goal, when we keep at the forefront of our minds the reason we are paying it. When we lose sight of the cause, the cost will always dominate and once that happens, it will dictate the agenda of how we live, what we live for and how much we're prepared to pay for it!

Ironically, Esau, Jacob's brother, lost sight of the *cause*, sacrificing his birthright for less than a Big Mac with fries!

Joseph kept sight of the *cause* as he said "No" to Potiphar's wife. He paid a high price to keep his integrity intact but it was worth it.

The rich young ruler lost sight of the *cause* and wasn't prepared to give what he had, to gain something far beyond the meagre boundaries of his great wealth.

The boy in the crowd saw the *cause* and gave his packed-lunch without hesitation. It was only small but didn't it go a long way?

For the joy set before Him, Jesus endured the cross, scorning the shame and paid the cost. He gladly accepted the burden of the sin of the world and paid an unimaginable price because He believed in and remained focused on the *cause* . . . on us!

Read slowly the words of Alexander Mackay a missionary to Uganda:

> "Within six months you will probably hear that one of us is dead. When the news comes do not be cast down; but send someone else immediately to take the vacant place."[2]

Though to some extent extreme, these or similar scenarios are played out regularly in our lives. Sometimes we become weary of the cost, especially when we lose sight of the cause, but if we can keep our eyes fixed on our purpose the price asked of us will always be affordable.

Jacob was able to work seven long years and make them seem like seven days, because he kept his eyes on the woman of his dreams. The vision of Rachel made the time fly and empowered him to pay the price for her love.

What dominates your thinking, *cause* or *cost*?

Investment or sacrifice?

> *"Jacob lay with Rachel also, and he loved Rachel more than Leah. And he worked for Laban another seven years."*

> (Genesis 29:30)

Imagine working seven years for the woman of your dreams and on your honeymoon waking up beside her sister! Not only would it be a shock, but the immense disappointment might be enough to cause you to give up on the dream. Not so Jacob. He's clearly upset, but his eyes are still on Rachel. He would not let her go and with unabated determination he agreed to another seven years of *investment*.

Jesus told the story of a man who was ploughing in a field. As he did so he discovered some treasure buried there. Jesus said the man immediately went, sold everything he had in order to buy the field so that in turn, he could have the treasure. Whatever the cost, he had to have the field. He knew in the light of the value of the treasure that the cost was an incredible investment, not a sacrifice.

One of the great tensions we have to hold is the balance between the temporal and the eternal. Paul put it this way:

"So we fix our eyes not on what is seen, but on what is unseen. For what is seen is temporary, but what is unseen is eternal."

(2 Corinthians 4:18)

If our focus is on the temporal, any cost we are asked to pay for the eternal will be viewed as a sacrifice. However, if our focus is on the eternal, any cost we are asked to pay in the temporal, will be viewed as an investment. Even though Jacob had been deceived (a taste of his own medicine no doubt), he still considered another seven years of work for Rachel not as a sacrifice, but as an investment. In his eyes, he was still getting a bargain. She was worth it, so the seven years extra, fourteen in total, were well worth paying.

The dictionary defines *sacrifice* as "the giving up of something for the sake of something else". It defines *invest* as "to spend (money, time etc.) on something with the expectation of profit".

Both words imply and in fact demand cost, but the *mind-sets* which govern both actions are poles apart. A sacrifice mentality can often be one dominated by loss-cost. Whereas an investment mentality is one motivated by return-cost: what will I get from this? Both give away and both make contributions, but one expects no return and therefore potentially sees any contribution as a loss, whereas the other expects a return in some capacity and therefore sees the cost as an investment.

We will never consistently cross the cost line if we're dominated by a warped understanding of sacrifice. Whatever God asks us to give up it is always with a view to some level of return. This is His nature and His law, for if we sow it, we'll reap it, sooner or later. I have often heard it said, "I don't give to get," and I know what is meant by that. But the truth is the Bible teaches that giving is a means to getting. If we sow, we will reap and if we give, it will be given back to us, *"pressed down, shaken together and running over"* (Luke 6:38). Our focus should not be on the getting, rather our energy should be on how and what we give. But at the same time we must not discount the value-added economy of the Kingdom of God which teaches us that for every investment, even if it is a cup of cold water given in His name, there will be a return.

So, what are you investing in? What cause are you giving yourself to?

Whether it is swimming the Channel, going to the Olympics, staying married to the same person for the rest of your life, raising children to play a dynamic role in their world or being part of a vibrant Christian community, cost must always be factored into the equation. However, if the *cause* dominates, Mach-busting breakthroughs await us and we'll always be willing and able to pay. Whatever we pay it will always be a worthwhile investment.

Success will never be cheap, but when we get to the other

side of the shaking, we'll discover that everything we gave for the *cause* was more than worth it. As one of my Mach-busting heroes so eloquently put it:

> "He is no fool who gives what he cannot keep, to gain that which he cannot lose."[3]

Notes

1. *Book of Firsts*, op. cit., pp. 26–27.
2. Kane, J., *A Concise History of the Christian World Mission* (Baker Academic, 1980), p. 98.
3. Jim Elliott, Journal entry October 28, 1949, Billy Graham Center Archives http://www.wheaton.edu/bgc/archives/faq/20.htm.

Lifting the Logic Lid

One of the first ways of preventing disease was to infect people with a weak strain of the disease itself to immunize them against catching a stronger deadlier strain. Known as inoculation or variolation, this idea was practised in the Middle and Far East long before it was introduced to Western Europe from Turkey in the early eighteenth century.

Dr Edward Jenner (of England) is famous for refining this process into a safer form, known as vaccination. Jenner's methods may not be considered ethical today; having infected eight-year-old James Phipps with cowpox to protect him against the deadly smallpox, Jenner later infected him with smallpox to prove that his theory worked.[1] Jenner was proved right and his system of "vaccination" was used to save countless lives.

We take immunization for granted now, except when the needle is being forced "gently" in our arm. I can't remember how many injections I've had for my travels, but imagine trying to explain to someone way back then, that the best way to prevent them getting a disease was in fact to give it to them first! This does not seem logical. To the average man in the street and indeed to many in the medical establishment, it would have seemed crazy!

Sometimes in order to break through to the next level, we have to have the courage to move beyond the conventional or known wisdom or logic of that moment, and dare to believe something else, which on the surface not only looks illogical, but a little weird or dangerous. A casual glance at the Bible shows such courage and breakthrough to be regular occurrences and already, in many of the examples we have looked at in this book, we can see this principle in play.

The dictionary defines logic as "the science of reasoning . . . a scheme of reasoning carrying conformity to its laws".

Every one of us has a logic we work to. Our upbringing, education, relationships, personality and belief all factor into *how we think*, how we conclude what we conclude. For example, if someone believes there is no God, then they must find answers to their questions without God being in the equation. That is their logic, their rationale, their system or scheme of thinking and this in turn will govern everything they do.

So what happens when what we are being challenged to do flies in the face of everything we know? That's the challenge of lifting the logic lid in our lives. This was the challenge facing Peter.

Take a moment to read Matthew 14:22–36

If Peter was to get out of the boat, a number of key areas of logic had to be overcome. Peter had a natural, "default" position in all of these areas and to get out of the boat and walk on water, if only for a few moments, everything would have to change.

The logic of feelings

Note the feelings which may have dominated Peter's mind and body as Jesus approached them that morning:

▶ **Fatigue**

> *"During the fourth watch . . . "*
>
> (Matthew 14:25)

That's 4:00 a.m. in the morning to me and you. (Yes, there are two four o'clocks!) These young men had been struggling most of the night and were exhausted. It's hard to accept the possibility of impossibility when you're shattered.

▶ **Fear**

> *" . . . they were terrified."*
>
> (Matthew 14:26)

In fact, they thought the figure walking to them on the water was a ghost. As we've seen already, if fear is allowed to dominate us it has the power to close our minds to the possibility of something new, dynamic or outside of our box and to convince us of the reality of something which is not true at all.

▶ **Confusion**

> *"Lord, if it's you . . . "*
>
> (Matthew 14:28)

Peter thought it was Jesus, but it seems he wasn't absolutely sure! *If* is such a small word, but it has huge implications. Peter wasn't sure hence the reason he asked the question. Uncertainty and confusion will strongly militate against us doing anything beyond the logic boundaries of our thinking.

Feelings play a big part in our lives; God created us to have feelings. But feelings should only ever serve us, never dominate us. The challenge comes when what we feel militates against what we need to or are being asked to do. Everything we feel at a given moment tells us it is wrong, yet we're confronted with the challenge to press forward. Peter was experiencing at least three strong emotions at a moment when he was being asked to step out of security into uncertainty. It wasn't ideal but it's what he had to deal with.

How many times do we start conversations with the question, "How are you?" It's a decent enough question. It's part of our system of polite etiquette, but it starts the conversation off from completely the wrong place. It invites feelings to be the driving factor of that encounter and feelings, whether high or low, usually dictate direction. Surely we must challenge ourselves to move to a place where what we believe and what we confess dictates even to how we feel.

There are days when I feel like a world-beater and other days when I feel like I've been beaten up by the world. That's how I feel – but what does the truth say? There are days when I feel like reading my Bible and others days when I don't. Sometimes I feel like praying and many times I don't. I brush my teeth every day … but I've never once felt like it! I eat bran for breakfast … seriously, who ever feels like doing that?! There are practices in my life, beliefs that I uncompromisingly hold to and people that I'm committed to that have nothing to do with how I feel. I have made decisions on all these areas regardless of the highs or lows of my life. I believe in Jesus whether I feel like it or not. I love my wife and children, whether I feel good or not. I give, whether I'm happy or not. My feelings factor in my life, but they don't master it!

We must not be afraid to embrace our feelings and our emotions, after all, God gave them to us, but if we're going to be Mach-busters, we can never allow how we feel to drive the agenda of our lives. We must be careful not to make decisions based simply on our fluctuating feelings. Our emotions and feelings must not dominate what we do, for there will be days when we have to do things that don't feel good or comfortable or right. Those are the moments that determine whether we Mach-bust and water-walk, or we stay in the boat with the life-jacket on.

"How do you feel about it?" That's the wrong question and it starts the journey from the wrong place. How you feel is important, but what's more important is what you *know* or *believe* about it!

The logic of experience

Nothing in Peter's library of experience could have prepared him for this moment. He had never seen or done anything like this before. There was no manual in the boat with a chapter heading, "What to do when asked to walk on water"! This was new territory and far beyond any boundaries that Peter had ever come close to. These were *uncharted waters* that Peter now found himself in and as far as experience was concerned . . . he was on his own!

When we are asked to do something for which we have no terms of reference, regardless of the scale of the task, it is one of the most challenging aspects of our lives. In such times we have nothing to fall back on, no memory bank to draw from and we may not even have friends who have gone this way either.

The logic of experience has a double edge.

▶ *Never tried that before!*
When I'm presented with a new challenge, I want to seek out people who have gone that way before in order to learn something from them on the issue. Over the years, I've come to realize that this can be incredibly helpful or painfully

restrictive and so I've become much more careful with regards to who I talk to. For example, pick a few mothers out of any group of people and ask them for their experience of having children and I guarantee the spectrum of what they've gone through will be incredible. Some will have "sailed through" pregnancy without any sickness or difficulties, with their baby "popping out" on time, leaving them with their pre-natal figure intact. (The women reading this book now know the author is a man.) Others will have had morning, afternoon, evening and middle of the night sickness, heartburn, swollen feet, weight gain and a labour that lasted longer than flying from London to Sydney and back. Who you listen to may determine whether you have a large family or choose to adopt!

If the water-walking moment is a completely new experience ... be careful who you talk to.

▶ *Been there, done that!*

Experience can be a hard lid to lift, especially the older we get because having been around a bit longer we naturally have more to compare it to. A previous positive experience for example, which may have a bearing on a present potential Mach-busting moment can help or hinder the step, depending on how we use that experience. Ironically because of our positive experience we can tend to think we know all there is to know about what is going to happen. The dangers here are apathy, over-confidence or even presumption. "Well, last time I walked on water it worked like this ... " Of course we must learn from experience, that's what it's there for but we must be careful not to allow even a previous *positive* experience to limit our responses to the things God is asking of us.

The other side of this coin, of course, is if the previous experience from which we draw was a negative one. "Last time I tried walking on water I realized I couldn't swim and I don't like a belly full of salty water!" This bad experience now stops us from trying again or from trusting God to do what He has promised. Many have promised themselves never to attempt water-walking again because of what happened the last time they tried. They remember the pain, embarrassment and disappointment, not to mention receiving mouth-to-mouth from the gentleman with bad breath and a spiky moustache.

I remember once using the phrase "You live and learn", to which a friend shot back, "Well, some people live and learn." The challenge is learning from the past (positive and negative) without allowing it to limit our present or future in any way. That's a tough one. I suppose the trick is to take each moment, each experience as it comes. To try and see, understand and respond to it on its own merits . . . drawing from whatever may be in the experience library but realizing that whatever is there may not be enough.

The logic of understanding

Before Peter climbed out of the boat, **he knew** this could not work. His intellect and understanding as a man and his profession as a fisherman told him that what he saw Jesus doing was impossible and that what he himself was now attempting to do was impossible. He knew it could not work, yet Jesus was asking him to come.

At this moment, two great schemes of reasoning clashed. Finite and infinite minds collided in this incredible moment of decision. Jesus knew stuff that Peter could not possibly understand, and without giving the young fisherman a Kingdom science lesson, He was asking Peter to trust, get out of the boat and walk. Peter had to "suspend" or override everything he knew, everything he had been taught and everything he had experienced in order to do what Jesus was asking of him!

> *"Trust in the* LORD *with all your heart*
>   *and lean not on your own understanding;*
> *In all your ways acknowledge him,*
>   *and he will make your paths straight."*

(Proverbs 3:5–6)

I like how the *Street Bible*[2] puts it:

> *"Base your confidence on God. Build your life on the girders God sets in place, not the flimsy scaffolding of your own good ideas. In everything you take on, put God top of the list of credits and He'll direct you."*

It sounds simple, until we have to put that into practice. It is no small thing when what God asks of us challenges all we know and have lived by and when He asks us to trust His intellect above our own in order to move us beyond the limitations of our knowledge. The only way that is possible is on the basis of trust. We have to come to a place where we trust God's knowledge more than our own! Isn't that ultimately what trust is? We place ourselves (whatever the circumstance) in the hands of another because we have confidence in their ability or knowledge to do what they have said.

In 2005 Christine left Rotherham, South Yorkshire, to work in Zimbabwe. Not only was she going at a time when Zimbabwe was experiencing political and economic upheaval, but she was working with its forgotten citizens – AIDS orphans. Just a few years previously, none of this would have seemed possible. Christine was nearly fifty, she was angry, in debt and going through a nasty divorce. In fact, she was fortunate to still have a boat, never mind to get out of one and walk on water. She lived for work, didn't like travelling and didn't care much for children. But when Jesus started to call her onto the water,

He asked her to give up her job, travel around the world and work with children. All of this was outside the experience boundary of Christine's life and none of it made sense. Thankfully she submitted her understanding to God's understanding, climbed out of her boat and in a Mach-busting decision, walked on water. Today, hundreds of lives have been changed because one woman lifted the lid of understanding and allowed God's logic to dictate the agenda.

Sometimes we miss great opportunities because what we know clashes with what God knows. If we win the logic argument with God, we'll most certainly never get out of the boat and the experience of walking on water will be for someone else to enthuse about over dinner.

None of this is easy of course – but by walking on water, for however long, Peter proved it was possible to lift the logic lid, to suspend how he felt as he overrode his experience library and surrendered his mind to a higher intelligence. If he can do it – then so can you!

Mach-busting, water-walking experiences await us all but they lie beyond the boundaries of the boat.

Notes _____

1. *Book of Firsts*, op. cit., pp. 172–173. Vaccination is so-called because the first vaccine was made from the cowpox virus *viriolae vaccinae* – *vacca* is the Latin for "cow".
2. *The Street Bible*, copyright © 2003 by Rob Lacey (Zondervan).

Short-term Gain or Long-term Glory?

Modern marathon runners are fortunate that they are not expected to emulate a feat accomplished by Pheidippides shortly *before* his famous run from Marathon to Athens. When the Persian army landed at Marathon, Pheidippides was sent to Sparta to ask for help to repel the invaders. He ran 150 miles in just two days! By the time the Spartans arrived at Marathon the Athenian army had won the battle without their help and Pheidippides was sent to Athens with news of the victory. He ran a further twenty-two miles without stopping and breathlessly delivered his message: "Rejoice, we conquer," just before he collapsed and died, probably from heat exhaustion.

The first organised race commemorating Pheidippides' amazing run was the Greek trial on 10th March 1896 for the first modern Olympic Games, which were to be held in Athens that same year; the course was that run by Pheidippides from Marathon to Athens. Interestingly, a modern marathon is 26 miles 385 yards. The reason for the odd length was that in the 1908 Olympics in London, the race began at Windsor Castle and had to finish in front of King Edward VII's royal box at the White City Stadium. The distance has stuck ever since.[1]

Pheidippides sacrificed his now for the future. He had a

vision and a passion beyond himself which allowed him to make decisions at great personal cost to himself. His sacrifice touched a nation, ensuring he would be immortalized as the original Marathon Man!

Sometimes, in order to break through into success and experience a Mach-busting moment, we have to sacrifice short-term gain for the prospect of long-term glory. This can be a difficult challenge because most of us are dominated by the *now*, by the need for immediate reward or satisfaction. We hate delayed gratification and our western society teaches us daily to expect nothing less than *now* fulfilment, an expectation that is neither realistic nor healthy. If we are going to be men and women who consistently live in the breakthrough, then we have to have a clear focus on the long-term – in our thinking and attitudes, we need to have a marathon mentality!

Moses was a marathon man – not only did he live long (120 years), but he lived well and throughout his life he was able to let go of the short-term in order to take hold of the long-term. This ability is celebrated in the hall of fame, which we call Hebrews 11.

Take a moment to read Hebrews 11:23–29.

From the simple statements contained in these verses, we can learn so much about living in the tension between the now and forever.

Moses teaches us that vision determines choices

Look at what Moses and his parents saw:

> "... because **they saw** he was no ordinary child ... "
>
> (Hebrews 11:23, emphasis added)

> "... **he was looking ahead** to his reward ... "
>
> (Hebrews 11:26, emphasis added)

"... he saw him who is invisible..."

(Hebrews 11:27, emphasis added)

Now look at what Moses and his parents did:

"... Moses' parents hid him for three months..."

(Hebrews 11:23)

"He regarded disgrace for the sake of Christ as of greater value than the treasures of Egypt..."

(Hebrews 11:26)

"... he left Egypt, not fearing the king's anger; he persevered..."

(Hebrews 11:27)

In each case, it was what either Moses or his parents saw, which determined the decisions they made and the choices they took. They saw things beyond what was going on around them. They could have had their eyes fixed on the king and his laws, the riches of Egypt and the opportunities so lavishly available. However, had their eyes been on those things, their decisions would have been very different.

It is crucial that we come to a revelation on a key and life-shaping fact – *vision determines choices.* That's why it is crucial for our vision to be on the right things. If our vision is *now* based, *gain* based, *comfort* based or *self* based, then we'll be more reluctant to make the sorts of decisions which will take us away from short-term gain and into long-term glory. We will tend to make choices that largely mean immediate results or quick gratification while neglecting the longer-term consequences and pay-off.

I once had a friend who had a world of opportunity before her. She was young, intelligent and gifted and the expanse that lay before her bore no comparison to the narrowness of her upbringing. Encouraged by her faith and her friends, she started to dip her toe into the sea of God-given possibilities that could have taken her far from the confines of mediocre village existence. That night in my kitchen, however, she attempted to convince me that the new man in her life, a non-Christian (who although he'd no interest in God "respected her faith"?) was the right way for her. She was convinced it would all work out fine. With as much love as I could muster I tried to warn this lovely young girl of the possible consequence of such a decision. But what did I know? Soon they were living together, a little later she was pregnant and not long after that, she was on her own ... with the baby. Today, she lives in the same village, shackled to a world much too small for her potential.

I share this not to judge but to challenge. If only at the moment of decision she could have seen beyond him, beyond need, beyond social and sexual pressure to all that she could have become. If only she could have glimpsed the children whose lives she would have helped change around the world. If only her eyes had been open to life beyond the limitation of her culture and history to see the glory of God's amazing purpose.

Moses *saw* the invisible, he *saw* his eternal reward and that empowered him to make choices which cost him in the short-term, but which paid off in the long-term.

> "Vision is everything. Your inner eyes of faith are your link between what is and all that will be!"[2]

It begs the question, what do *you* see?

Moses teaches us that purpose determines expectations

> *"By faith Moses, when he had grown up, refused to be known as the son of Pharaoh's daughter. He chose to be ill-treated along with*

the people of God rather than to enjoy the pleasures of sin for a short time."

(Hebrews 11:24–25)

Why would anyone choose to be ill-treated when a life of luxury was on offer?

▶ *Purpose!*

As Moses grew up, he discovered his purpose. This discovery in turn empowered him to move his "gratification-base" away from personal gratification to purpose gratification. He could have expected a life of self-indulgent excess but once he discovered his purpose, he knew that his choices would prevent this. Accordingly, he changed his expectations of life and what he thought he would get out of it, and aligned his expectations with purpose, knowing there would be a reward for him. Moses moved his expectations away from his Egyptian world, to a world dominated by the purpose of God. Therefore when it came to letting go of all that Egypt offered, its short-term pleasures and rewards, he was both willing and able to do so, because his expectations had changed.

Whatever our vision-based choices are, our expectations must align themselves accordingly.

We cannot, and should not, expect the rewards that Egypt offers if we're going to leave. We cannot expect an easy ride if we've not learned to drive. If we're going to rock the boat and disturb the way things have always been done we have to expect problems. We cannot expect the privilege of a son of Egypt when we no longer want to be one. Moses knew that once he made his decision he would no longer be afforded the luxury of Egypt and so he adjusted his expectations accordingly. Not once do we hear him complain about his lack or his life in the desert or what he missed about Egypt – he let it go and adjusted his expectations to align with his choices and moved on.

Expectations need to be handled wisely. On the one hand they can be an expression of faith and hope but on the other they can become hard task-masters enslaving us to aspirations that will never be realized.

▶ *Unadjusted expectations*

Having had the privilege of leading a number of missions teams to many nations around the world I sometimes find people falling into the "It's not like home" syndrome. Confronted with different food, climate and culture some have stated the obvious, "It's not like England!" There is one simple response, "That's because it's not England!" If a person is to travel successfully, they must understand that the world where they got on the plane will be different from the one where they leave it. Life is a whole lot easier when we adjust our expectations to accommodate the new challenge. This does not mean a person has to drop their standards or put up with mediocrity, but it does mean appropriating what we believe to the reality of what is being faced. Too many want to experience "home from home" when they travel. If this is our expectation, my question has to be, why travel?

Failure to adjust expectations can be painful and dangerous. Adjustment does not mean abandonment or compromise, but if we expect five-star treatment in a $5 a night hotel, we'll be disappointed for sure and that disappointment may cause us to lose sight of our expectations altogether.

▶ *Unrealistic expectations*

The X Factor was an opportunity for thousands of pop-star wannabes to have a go at winning a £1 million recording contract. People could literally walk in off the street and try to persuade a panel of judges to give them a chance of glory. I likened the programme to driving past a motorway crash, "I know I shouldn't look, but I can't help myself." Watching men and women of all ages shapes and sizes strut their stuff in the hope that they had the X factor swung from being inspiring to frightening. The sad thing was that many who walked in the room really believed they could sing; that they would be the next big thing. Listening to their talk they were convincing, but listening to them singing was horrifying. Unrealistic expectations can be unforgivingly cruel.

Some people have been broken by the sheer pressure of carrying the burden of expectations that they were never designed to bear. Unrealistic expectations have convinced them that they can, when really they can't. They believe they should have a go, when wisdom dictates they step back. Imagine trying to convince an acorn that it can grow to be an apple. This would be crazy. Yet because of a "word from God" a *captain of fifty* has an unrealistic expectation that he can be a captain of a thousand and is killing himself in the process. A church that has numbered thirty for the last fifty years has an unrealistic expectation that three thousand will be added to them in the next year! God can do anything ... but we can't! If you're an acorn then have an expectation to be the best oak tree you can be. If you're a captain of fifty, make the fifty feel like they're the most important people in the world.

▶ *Unfulfilled expectations*
The Royal Marines are an elite fighting unit in the British army. One of the maxims they are taught throughout their training is, "There's one thing you can count on in a battle situation, things will never go according to plan." They call it "Dislocated Expectations" and they are trained not only to expect it but how to prepare for and overcome it. For them it may literally be the difference between life and death.[3]

How we cope when life doesn't work out just as we expected can make the difference between a Mach-busting moment or meltdown. Some have walked away from ministries, marriages, jobs and friendships because what they expected didn't happen. I heard of a family impacted by a big win on the lottery. The winner generously gave gifts to the various members of their family, some receiving as much as £10,000. Incredibly, some family members were upset because they had expected more. Had they been told that before the day was over they'd be £10,000 richer they would have been over-joyed but because they were expecting £100,000, they were disappointed!

Your dream hasn't quite worked out. The marriage didn't last. Your children don't call often. Your job wasn't what you'd hoped for. Your body doesn't work as well it should. All of these things (and much more) are examples of unfulfilled or dislocated expectations. Such disappointment can crush the spirit and wear us down. If that's how you feel, Job felt the same way. In a very short period of time, all he had built and worked for was cruelly snatched away and to make his anguish worse, his three "friends" seemed to take great delight in telling him it was all his fault! Job struggled, but in the midst of it all he found strength by going back to his rock-like foundations and holding on with all his strength.

> *"I know that my Redeemer lives,*
>   *and that in the end he will stand upon the earth.*
> *And after my skin has been destroyed,*
>   *yet in my flesh I will see God;*
> *I myself will see him*
>   *with my own eyes – I, and not another.*
>   *How my heart yearns within me!"*

(Job 19:25–27)

Many want to live in the joy of purpose and the pulse of vision whilst holding on to expectations that they can still retain benefits from alternative choices. They expect to make hard choices and have an easy life. They expect to stand up for righteousness and not catch a little flak. They expect to lead and never be hurt, or serve without ever being misunderstood. They expect to do the will of God without cost and pain! I am not saying we must expect the worst, but simply that our expectations must align themselves with the reality of the choices we make. Don't get me wrong, God is awesome and He will see to it that you get everything you need when you put Him first. We can expect all our needs to be met, for our children to be mighty in the land and for our lives to experience overwhelming blessing – but it just won't be Egyptian style! You'll get God's reward and the glory. It just might look a little different from Pharaoh's!

Moses teaches us that faith determines values

> *"He regarded disgrace for the sake of Christ as of greater value than the treasures of Egypt . . . "*
>
> (Hebrews 11:26)

Note the phrase "greater value". Faith was what elevated disgrace to a higher value than treasures and riches. What we value is a direct reflection of what we believe and believe in. If you value something, it is because you truly believe it to be valuable. It plays a useful role in your life. Purpose-filled faith will determine what gets pre-eminence in our value system. What we believe about our purpose will determine what we truly value and hold to be special in our life. Though Moses had fully enjoyed the wealth, privilege and influence of his position in Egypt, he realized it was not his purpose. Consequently, his belief system changed and with it, his value system. That which once he would have fought to preserve, he gladly and unhesitatingly gave away. That's what purpose-filled faith will do!

Shammah was the third of the top three of David's mighty men (along with Josheb-Basshebeth and Eleazar). Shammah is famed for defending a field full of lentils. We're not even sure it was his field but it was in that field he decided to take a faith stand and defend what he believed in.

> *"But Shammah took his stand in the middle of the field. He defended it and struck the Philistines down . . ."*
>
> (2 Samuel 23:12)

An ordinary field of lentils is important to us because Shammah's faith saw something of value in it. He was prepared to fight, kill and even die for this field because his faith filled it with importance.

I wonder, is there anything in your life worth living, giving and fighting for? If everyone else is running away, is there a principle, a person, or a purpose for which you by faith would take a stand? When you do take that stand, you just might experience a Mach-busting victory.

Consider the occasion when Jesus healed a woman on the Sabbath (see Luke 13:10–17, *Message*):

> *"He [Jesus] was teaching in one of the meeting places on the Sabbath. There was a woman present, so twisted and bent over with arthritis that she couldn't even look up. She had been afflicted with this for eighteen years."*

What happened next was truly remarkable, because Jesus was in the same meeting place. He did six incredible things:

1. **He saw her.**

   What's so remarkable about that? She was not only a woman sitting separate from the men, but she was a crippled and unlovely woman, but Jesus noticed her.

2. **He called her.**

   Men and women never mixed in public and in the place of worship care was taken to ensure that the sexes were segregated. Jesus called her into the male area.

3. **He spoke to her.**

   "Woman, you're free!" It was bad enough to call her over, but then He broke all cultural etiquette by speaking to her.

4. **He touched her.**

   Most shocking of all, Jesus reached out and physically engaged with the woman. She probably hadn't been touched tenderly by anyone for as long as she could remember, but Jesus did.

5. **He healed her.**

   Ironically this was the thing which upset the leader of the meeting the most. He felt that it was wrong to heal someone on God's day! His religiousness led him to foolishness.

6. **He elevated her.**

   Jesus was challenged on His actions and in defending Himself, He subtly inserted a remarkable phrase when referring to the woman. He called her a *"daughter of Abraham."*

Jesus valued this woman so much that He was prepared to break social and religious convention, attack cultural taboos and wage spiritual war. To most she was a useless, crippled woman, of little value to anyone, but to Jesus, she was a daughter of Abraham. As He later gloriously announced:

> *"For the Son of Man came to seek and to save what was lost."*
>
> (Luke 19:10)

"Ah, that's Jesus", I hear you say! You're right, it is Jesus, but it's also a demonstration of faith that finds value in someone who would ordinarily be abandoned to the scrap heap. Because Jesus valued her, He fought for her, gave to her and transformed her. Jesus was prepared to break through the barriers, creating a Mach-busting moment because He found someone worth doing it for.

We will always settle for the ease of the short-term gain at the expense of the long-term glory when we lose sight of what is truly valuable and important. We are all tempted by the path of least resistance, by the allure of fast result options, but there are few short-cuts to most places worth going to. Like Moses, Jesus was offered some very attractive short-cuts. He was offered everything any man would want or desire, pain free; all He had to do was let go of the long-term glory beyond the cross and take the soft option put before Him. But thanks be to God, Jesus looked beyond the now and saw something much more glorious than anything on offer.

> *"In bringing many sons to glory, it was fitting that God, for whom and through whom everything exists, should make the author of their salvation perfect through suffering."*
>
> (Hebrews 2:10)

Mach-busting moments aren't cheap or easy but the long-term success of decisions based on vision, purpose and faith far outweigh any gain that a brief moment of easy gratification may have promised. Moses ran an amazing marathon and broke through seemingly impossible barriers. His life inspires us to ensure that long-term glory always eclipses any short-term gain.

Notes

1. *Book of Firsts*, op. cit., pp. 244–245.
2. Gilpin, D., *Jesus, Save Me from Your Followers* (New Wine Press, 2006), p. 13.
3. Woodward, C., *Winning* (Hodder & Stoughton, 2004), p. 241.

CHAPTER 7

History Does Not Determine Destiny

A new young monk arrived at the monastery. He was assigned to help the other monks in copying the old canons and laws of the church by hand. He noticed, however, that all the monks were copying from copies and not from the original manuscript. So he went to the head abbot to question this practice, pointing out wisely that if someone made even a small error in the first copy, it would never be picked up. In fact, that error would be continued in all of the subsequent copies. The head monk responded, "We have been copying from the copies for centuries, but you make a good point my son."

So the abbot went down into the dark caves underneath the monastery where the original manuscripts were stored in a locked vault that hadn't been opened for hundreds of years. Hours went by and nobody saw or heard anything from him.

Eventually, the young monk became worried and ventured to look for him. When he found the abbot he saw him banging his head against the wall repeatedly and wailing, "We forgot the R, we forgot the R!" By this time his forehead was bloody and bruised and he was crying uncontrollably. Calming the abbot down a little, the young monk asked, "What's the matter,

Father? What is the problem with the R?" With a choking voice
the old abbot replied, "The word is CELEBRATE!"

The past can have a profound impact on our present and
future if we grant it permission to do so. Many believe that the
circumstances of their history determine the outcome of their
destiny, but this is not what the Bible teaches. Yesterday's
mistakes do not have to set the pattern for tomorrow. Yesterday's limitations do not have to set the boundaries for tomorrow.

When George Washington Carver, a professor at Alabama's
Tuskegee Institute suggested that cotton farmers in Alabama
County switch from growing cotton to peanuts, most people
thought he was crazy. Endless cotton crops had drained the land
of nutrients, but Carver suggested that peanuts as well as sweet
potatoes, cowpeas and soybeans would restore nitrogen and
fertility to the soil. However, he could not convince the farmers.
In 1915 a plague of boll weevils ravaged the area and Carver
suggested that they burn the infested cotton and plant peanuts.
Out of necessity they did and soon, with barns overflowing, had
more peanuts than they could cope with. With some inspiration
from heaven, Carver set to work night and day to unlock the
qualities of the peanut, and eventually during his lifetime he
extracted more than three hundred products from it. In just five
years, peanut production turned his Alabama County into one
of the wealthiest sections of the state.[1]

Say it out loud – *"My history does not determine my destiny!"*

His father was a hard-working dairy farmer in Charlotte, North
Carolina, and at 2:30 a.m. (yes, that's a.m.) he would wake
his boys for their chores on the farm. His youngest, Melvin,
loved the work but the eldest, Billy Frank, struggled. At every
opportunity, he would retreat to the hayloft and read whatever
books he could get his hands on. He was expected to be a dairy

farmer like his dad, yet Billy soon left home and went on to touch the world. His family and friends knew him as Billy Frank, but the world knows him as Billy Graham, a man who devoted his life to sowing and reaping a different kind of harvest.[2]

Say it out loud – *"My history does not determine my destiny!"*

History was the immense challenge facing a young man called Jabez. His name and story are contained in the midst of a long list of other names and genealogies. It's easy to miss this jewel buried under layers of apparent routine but there he is, screaming a message of hope and victory, a Mach-busting insertion begging for our attention.

Read it for yourself in 1 Chronicles 4:9–10.

See the details of his past:

> *"His mother had named him Jabez, saying, 'I gave birth to him in pain.'"*

(verse 9)

That sounds harmless enough, until we discover the meaning of the name *Jabez*. It can mean "sorrow", "trouble" or "grief". Some have literally translated it *pain*. It seems that because his mother gave birth to him in pain (and we're not sure what that pain was), she decided that forever her son would be reminded of that fact every time she called him. What a tragedy that she allowed her pain to affect and infect the life of another human being. I once heard an old pastor say, "Hurt people hurt people." In this case, the maxim certainly holds.

Perhaps we could pause for just a moment and consider this. Be careful not to allow the pain and hurt we have suffered become a mantle we place on others. Maybe you were neglected or wounded by your parents. I urge you, don't let your children suffer your pain. Could it be someone cheated on you, left your marriage high and dry? I encourage you, don't let your relationships suffer your pain. Perhaps someone let you down. Don't make your hurt and pain a "gift" to those you seek to serve. Jabez's mother did her son a huge disservice by blaming him for her pain. Thankfully Jabez discovered that his history did not determine his destiny!

Our past is undeniable, but the glorious truth about the past is that *it is in the past!* The reality is that whatever has happened to us, or whatever our experience may have been, it is behind us, it is in our past. However, the Mach-busting moment comes when we decide to leave the limitation of our past and press on into the future God has for us. We have a choice to carry the past around with us as a constant reminder of what has been, or we can face it, accept it, and leave it behind. Our past will always be part of our history, but it does not have to be part of our today or our tomorrow! We make the choice.

> "You will never collide with your destiny if you are trapped in a continuous cycle of thought patterns, lifestyle choices and negative habits dictated by your background. You do not have to be a victim of your past."[3]

The pain of Jabez's past threatened to become a prophecy of his future. So how did he break through the shakes of his own personal history to discover the success of his destiny? What set him apart, so that he became *"more honourable than his brothers"* (v. 9)?

He refused to play the blame-game

On 23rd September 1961, Brian Gault was born with no arms, a victim of the drug thalidomide, prescribed to help relieve his mother's morning sickness.

"At my birth, my parents were offered several alternatives regarding my upbringing – none of them the option of keeping me and raising me at home. Institutionalisation was deemed suitable for a child born without arms – or perhaps adoption ... but the thought that my parents might love me and want to keep me did not enter the equation."

Who would have thought this baby would have survived? This baby with no arms became a preacher with a mission to touch those branded hopeless. He travelled the world and now has a family of his own. He continues to be an inspiration to thousands of people. Brian's own words are ample conclusion on the matter,

"I believe that God will use my disability to help others come to faith in the God who never makes mistakes. He made me without arms for a purpose and I trust he will use me to take his love to those whom he has also created to be 'different'." [4]

What don't you hear in that statement? Blame. No doubt, someone was to blame and ultimately should be brought to account for this tragedy, but Brian made a decision to move beyond blame and get on with his life, and what a life he's lived!

In the few words attributed to Jabez, there is not even a hint of blame towards his mother. If we entered the passage at verse 10, we would have no idea of the pain and hurt that had preceded these words. Jabez was not looking for someone to blame, he was looking for blessing. Whatever his mother did or didn't do, Jabez refused to hide behind his hurt and resisted the temptation to beat her with the baton of blame. Jabez did not play the blame-game.

What happens when we play the blame-game?

▶ *It gives us an excuse to fail*

"It's not my fault if I fail ... I'm like this or this happened because..." It is convenient to find something or someone to blame for our own failure. It releases us from having to take responsibility for our own actions; after all, we argue, they are the product of other things and the actions of other people. Though this is the easiest route, it will not only affirm us as residents of victimsville, but it will ensure that every journey ends up in a dead-end street.

▶ *We become part of the problem not part of the solution*

The blame-game ties us into a never-ending cycle that only ever spirals down, never up. Our attitude feeds this ravenous black hole without ever satisfying it. The more we play, the stronger it becomes and we find that our attitude becomes as much part of the problem as the original problem in the first place. This can be a killer.

▶ *We win but always lose*

If we want someone or something to blame, we'll never be disappointed. We'll always win in our pursuit of fault. Pastors, churches, spouses, parents and our environment are easy targets, and if all else fails, there's always the government. The funny thing is, even when we find someone to blame we still lose. Nothing gets solved or fixed and we're never really satisfied with the outcome. Even when our blame hits the target, somehow victory eludes us.

Jabez refused to live under the shadow of blame and instead settled in the land of blessing. We can too, but we must choose to do so and let go of blame. Perhaps it is time to face the past, forgive the past and let go of it once and for all. Leave your past where it belongs, in the past and press on into the glorious future that awaits you. Why live in blame when you can live in blessing? Let it go and live!

He looked up not back

This is summed up in the expression: *"Jabez cried out to the God of Israel . . . "* (1 Chronicles 4:10).

Through revelation, Jabez came to a life-transforming understanding that the only way out of his limitation was not to look back but to look up. He understood that only God could bless him in the way he needed, that only God could enlarge his territory beyond the limitation of his past and that only God could keep him from harm and bring freedom from pain.

Looking up, he learned to confess and ask for the right things and as a result, heaven moved on his behalf and the Bible declares: *"God granted his request"* (v. 10).

Our history, whatever it is, will never be able to determine our destiny if our vision and focus is upward and forward. Looking back will not only give us a pain in the neck, we'll become a pain in the neck. Looking back will take the energy required for living today and use it on a life already gone, pain already experienced, anger already expressed and tears already shed. You did that then, why keep doing it today? This could be the moment when you stop looking back and start looking up.

A friend of mine wrote a poem which expressed this experience like this:

I'm the ghost of a not-dead man,
A waste of space, an also-ran.
A failed attempt at something great,
A player caught in fool's mate.
A man who saw the truth, and yet,
Risked everything and lost the bet.

A swine who took his pearls,
And cast them in to sinking sand.
A battery, flat, a dieter, fat,
An eaten hat, a deaf bat, a dead cat,
A pointless, worthless, careless,
      loveless good-for-nothing rat.

But

I'm the child of a not-dead God,
Who comforts me with staff and rod.
Whose love will never ever end,
And in whose hands I'll break and mend.
And who, despite our flaws intends,
Into this broken world to send.
Such punched-up, patched-up, stitched-up,
      love-struck ragamuffin men.[5]

This is one of the few times you can truly say with me, thank God for a **big but**!

It's the *but* in this poem which makes all the difference. It's the moment when a man turns his eyes from a backward fixation to an upward focus. Looking back will always leave us consumed with what might have been, who we might have been, what could or should have been, but looking up fills us with the glorious faith-filled possibility that more can happen, life goes on and that life isn't over yet.

Somebody once said:

> "Man can live about forty days without food, about three days without water, about eight minutes without air, but only for seconds without hope."[6]

What will happen if we keep looking back and not up?

▶ *We'll find it almost impossible to go forward with purpose*
Try cutting the lawn while looking behind and see what
happens. Nice straight lines you will not have. Forward movement is possible even if our eyes are focusing on what is behind
us, but intentional, purpose-filled forward movement is virtually impossible. Perhaps God has given us a clue about vision
through our own anatomy by placing our eyes in the *front* of
our head. Sometimes people express, "If only I had eyes in the
back of my head." I know what they mean but I'm glad God
hasn't granted that wish. Eyes in the back of our head would
mean preoccupation with what is behind us instead of what is
in front of us. As I drive my car, three mirrors assist me to
glance at what is behind to increase my awareness, but if
my journey is going to be successful my main focus must be
ahead.

▶ *We'll miss what is right in front of us*
Recently, my son Simeon and I watched a soccer match in
which England played Andorra in a European Championship
qualifying clash. England won 5–0 and Simeon missed every
goal! Why? He was looking at other things. To be fair, it's hard
for a nine-year-old to sit through a ninety-minute game, but
what are the chances of missing all five goals? It's possible to
miss what is right in front of us, to miss what we're really
looking for because our eyes are focused on other things. The
preoccupation of the piece of spinach between your spouse's
teeth may cause you to miss the beauty of their eyes and the
dirt on the face of your children might distract you from their
smile. It's easily done and happens to all of us every day. That's
why we must make a conscious decision about what we look at.
Preoccupation with yesterday will cause us to miss the beauty
and possibilities of the day right in front of us. Hanging on to
yesterday's offence will distract us from the generosity of a

friend today. Rehearsing past failure will always take our eyes away from what is and what could be, to what was!

▶ *A collision is inevitable*

Have you ever bumped into something because you weren't looking where you were going? I have, we've probably all done it. Any parents reading this will have dozens of such experiences to recount to their children. Mention the word *Ulsterbus* and a shudder of embarrassment still overcomes me. I was a teenager on my way from Belfast to Bangor. A large queue of people was waiting to get on and I was right at the back. As I was about to get on, I was distracted and looked behind me while still moving forward. As I turned around to face the driver and pay my fare, the doors began to close and (I'm telling the truth) I got my head stuck between the doors. My cry (and possibly bulging eyeballs) alerted the driver and he immediately opened the doors while offering a continual apology. I was greeted on the packed bus by a mixture of applause and laughter (and just one old dear asking, "Are you all right son?") Of course it was no-one's fault but mine, although I did hope for divine judgment on the driver. I wasn't looking where I was going and when that happens, collision is inevitable.

It is no surprise to me that those whose eyes are fixed on their history and especially its pain or failure, keep bumping into things, usually resulting in more pain and hurt. It's time to take our eyes off the past and, as we've said in an earlier chapter, strain forward. If we don't, more pain, disappointment and limitation await us in the future, but it doesn't have to be that way. Today, we can make decisions and pray prayers that can make a Mach-busting difference to our lives.

Jabez refused to play the blame-game and let his vision be dominated by his past. Instead, he released what had been and reached out to what could be. His ambitions for the future superseded the limitation of his past and he refused to allow his history to dictate and determine his destiny. Jabez speaks and we need to listen. He broke through the shakes of his history and so can we.

Notes

1. Lucado, M., *Cure for the Common Life* (W Publishing Group, 2005), pp. 11–12.
2. Graham, B., *Just as I Am* (HarperCollins, 1977).
3. Houston, B., *Get a Life* (STL, 2000).
4. Gault, B. (with Helena Rogers), *Look, No Hands!* (Hodder & Stoughton, 2000), pp. 3–4, 202.
5. Matthew Saunders, 2006.
6. Anonymous. Quoted in David Shearman, *Hope Against All Odds* (New Wine Press, 2006), p. 12.

CHAPTER 8

The Art of
Self-Encouragement

"It always seems to me that we are trying anxiously in this way
to reserve some space for God; I should like to speak of God
not on the boundaries but at the centre, not in weaknesses but
in strength; and therefore not in death and guilt but in man's
life and goodness."

These defiant, hopeful and faith-filled words were written by
Dietrich Bonhoeffer to a friend, from his prison cell in 1944.
Bonhoeffer, a Lutheran theologian and pastor, had been one of
the few German Church leaders who spoke out against the
persecution of the Jews by the Nazis. It was his passion for
the German people and for peace which led him to become
involved in a plot to assassinate Adolf Hitler; a stand which
many German Christians neither understood nor forgave. He
was arrested for "high treason and treason against one's
country". Imprisonment and interrogation became his way of
life, but in it all, somehow, Bonhoeffer retained his dignity and
his faith. Each day was made bearable by his faith. "The Bible
provided support, and recollected hymns provided comfort."

Despite Allied bombing raids, a shortage of food and the
cruelty of prison guards, Bonhoeffer was able somehow to
see "forces of good" at work and found the courage to face

his circumstances. In one letter to his fiancée Maria von Wedemeyer, he included a poem entitled, *By the Powers of Good*. The last stanza expresses his faith:

> "The forces of good surround us in wonder,
> They firm up our courage for what comes our way.
> God's with us from dawn to the slumber of evening,
> The promise of love at the break of each day."

Others saw this gentle pastor's faith and resolve shine through. Captain Payne Best of the British Secret Service met Dietrich while in Buchenwald concentration camp in 1945 and commented, "Bonhoeffer was different; just quite calm and normal, seemingly perfectly at ease ... his soul really shone in the dark desperation of our prison." As he left Captain Best, Bonhoeffer's parting words were, "This is the end – for me the beginning of life."

A few months later on 9th April, 1945 at Flossenburg, the prison doctor watched as Dietrich knelt in prayer before facing his execution. "I was most deeply moved by the way this lovable man prayed, so devout and so certain that God heard his prayer." He prayed again as he approached the gallows, and then he climbed the steps, "brave and composed".[1]

I don't know about you, but I am both challenged and inspired by this story. Whatever we think of Bonhoeffer's actions, we cannot argue with the resolve and determination he so clearly demonstrated during a period of intense crisis. Somehow Bonhoeffer found a way to encourage himself in God to such a degree that he looked out for the needs of others and not just his own. As a prisoner of Finkenwalde observed, "... during air raids, and during the exercises in the yard, Bonhoeffer became the pastor of his fellow prisoners, and even, increasingly, of his warders."[2]

Dietrich became a Mach-buster in the harsh reality of Germany's concentration camps. Finding hope and strength, he not only encouraged himself but he encouraged others. Is such a thing possible, to live beyond the boundaries of a prison cell? Both the Bible and Bonhoeffer's experience tell us it is, so . . . read on!

Take a moment to read 1 Samuel 30:1–6.

This is an amazing episode in the life of David. One statement stands out:

> "But David found strength in the LORD his God."
>
> (1 Samuel 30:6)

The Amplified Bible puts it like this:

> " . . . but David encouraged and strengthened himself in the Lord his God."

The phrase which the NIV translates *"found strength"* is an incredibly powerful one. It can mean "to fasten upon, to seize and be strong". Here it points to the idea of David *fastening himself* to God, *seizing onto Him* and consequently encouraging and strengthening himself. In the midst of a life-threatening crisis, David took hold of God and experienced an immense Mach-busting moment which probably saved not only his life, but also that of his men and their families.

But how does someone "encourage" or "strengthen" themselves in the Lord?

Get into God's presence

When David and his men returned to their camp, they discovered the Amalekites had done a "David on David". Raiding the camp, they took everything including women and children. The reaction of David and his men was natural:

> *"So David and his men wept aloud until they had no strength left to weep."*
>
> (1 Samuel 30:4)

But what happened next was dangerous:

> *"... each one was bitter in spirit because of his sons and daughters."*
>
> (1 Samuel 30:6)

Grief is one thing, bitterness is something else. Bitterness will take grief into anger and anger fully grown can lead to rebellion and revenge. David's mighty men started to crumble. In just a few moments they went from loyal warriors to willing assassins. David's life was in danger because his men had allowed their spirits to become disconnected from God and the result was potentially devastating. They no longer remembered what God had done nor could they see that God was still able to give them success. Instead, bitterness caused them to focus entirely on their own pain and loss with the very real possibility that in a moment of anger they might destroy all that God had purposed for them through the anointed leadership of David. They were not thinking straight because their spirits were bent out of shape by bitterness.

A word of advice: when everyone around you is losing their head and blaming it on you ... *run to the presence of God!* It was within the context of David's mighty men going into spiritual meltdown that the Bible records David's definitive breakthrough. When everyone was out of control, David got connected!

> *"But David found strength in the LORD his God."*

When we have the courage to reconnect with the presence of God, it's amazing how our perspective on life changes. Just ask Asaph. He was a Levite, appointed over the service of praise in the time of David and Solomon. He led the singing and sounded cymbals before the Ark of God, and there are twelve psalms credited to him. One of them, Psalm 73, gives us an insight into the condition of the heart of this man of God:

> *"But as for me, my feet had almost slipped;*
> *I had nearly lost my foothold.*
> *For I envied the arrogant*
> *when I saw the prosperity of the wicked."*

(Psalm 73:2–3)

For whatever reason, Asaph took his eyes off God and began to look at the "live it large" lifestyle of the sinners around him. He noticed that even though they were up to their armpits in sin, they had big houses, fast transport, fine clothes, vintage wine and villas on the coast. I can almost sense the Porsche, the Rolex and the Lear jet. His spirit became bitter, bordering on rebellion as he reached his lowest point:

> *"Surely in vain have I kept my heart pure;*
> *in vain have I washed my hands in innocence."*

(Psalm 73:13)

Are these the words of the sweet singer, who helps the people to worship the King of the universe? Bitterness of spirit threatens to permanently evict this man from the presence of God. He was on his way out until something radically changed:

> *"When I tried to understand all this,*
> *it was oppressive to me*

> *till I entered the sanctuary of God;*
> *then I understood their final destiny."*

(Psalm 73:16–17)

God's presence gave Asaph perspective. The world looked different when viewed from God's presence and at that moment, he not only understood, but he gained insight into his own stupidity. Listen to his conclusion:

> *"When my heart was grieved*
> *and my spirit embittered,*
> *I was senseless and ignorant;*
> *I was a brute beast before you."*

(Psalm 73:21–22)

They are strong words but they are the truth. How many times has rubbish come out of my mouth or have I heard nonsense come out of the mouths of others when we have allowed bitterness to reign and entice us away from the sacred and lovely presence of God?

The art of self-encouragement begins with a trip into the presence of God. It's the safest place to run to and live in when the pressure of life intimidates. Don't loiter at the entrance go straight in, for when we enter His presence so much will change. His presence enables us to understand the truth and see things differently, and that is what can make all the difference.

Get back to God's promise

David could hear what his men were saying. Had he listened to them, it would all have been over. David needed some advice, a word from another source. So what does he do? While his men are plotting his downfall, David calls for the priest and enquires of the Lord. We're not absolutely certain whether David took the ephod and enquired of the Lord for himself or whether he went through Abiathar. Either way, he asked, and even more importantly, God answered! David was re-energised and on the strength of what God said went forward, taking his so-called mighty men with him. He needed a word and in the presence of God, he was given one.

We could learn from David here. So often when we are confronted with a barrier to our progress we listen to the grumblers, the dissenters and the complainers. The people who tell us we cannot, we will not or we should not. Listening to such advice will root us to negativity and faith will rise to the dizzy heights of our toenails. My mother-in-law has a fridge magnet slogan which asks, "How can I fly like an eagle when I am surrounded by turkeys?" It's not in the Bible and it isn't the whole truth but it does contain some sense. If we listen to the words of the embittered it won't exactly inspire us to fly up to the heights!

At such times we would do well to *call for a priest* and *enquire of the Lord*. It is interesting that in the midst of David's crisis he called for a man of God to assist him in finding the mind of God for his situation. Part of the art of self-encouragement is to know who and what to listen to. I'm not saying we have to find a priest, but what I am saying is that in order to get through times of crisis and become a Mach-buster, we have to learn to discern who and what is good for us. Some would rather seek "wisdom" from the chat-shows, the tabloids or their mate at work who doesn't know the first thing about walking with God. Don't be spiritually stupid – grow up and learn to listen to the word of God.

I love the story of Abraham. It has everything in it, courage, love, betrayal, doubt, pain, prosperity and a happy ending. God gives us a "warts and all" exposé of this man of God and his journey. He had many low points and some incredible high points, but in the end he makes it and stands today as the father of all who believe. Paul gives us insight into some of the challenges this man faced telling us that Abraham's body was as good as dead and that Sarah's womb was dead also. Yet Abraham and Sarah held the son of promise. Paul sums it up when he states:

> *"Against all hope, Abraham in hope believed and so became the father of many nations, just as it had been said to him, 'So shall your offspring be.'"*

(Romans 4:18)[3]

Abraham was able to continue in hope and faith. Why? Because of the Word that had been given to him. When God first promised, *"So shall your offspring be,"* Abraham had no idea how or when it would work out, but in it all, through the failures, the false starts and the long years of waiting, he held onto the Word and the Word did not let him down.

If we want to live in the power of self-encouragement then we must get the Word, hold on to the Word, believe the Word and do the Word. Then, no weapon formed against us will prosper and we'll experience the delight of Mach-busting moments.

Get on with God's purpose

The picture is now changing for David. A few moments previously, the world looked a dangerous place. Grief and bitterness had threatened to destroy everything, but David's decision to reconnect with God, call for the man of God and listen to the Word of God changed everything. David now knew exactly what to do and was confident that God was in it.

Revitalised by the Word, David returns to his men with an encouraged spirit and gives them all a way out of their despair. He leads his six hundred men back into the fight and the amazing thing is, he and his men not only got back what had been taken from them, but they were able to take plunder from their enemy as well. God had turned a devastating attack into an opportunity of overflowing prosperity – but it could have been so different.

I have a saying that hangs on the wall of my office:

> A leader was asked the question, "What is the key to success?"
> "Doing the right thing . . . long enough." He answered.

I like that. One of the major keys to living in the power of self-encouragement is to continue to do the things we know we ought to do. Yet, if we're honest, when pressure or pain comes, the last thing we feel like doing is serving, giving or going the extra mile. All we want to do is withdraw, wrap our hands around an extra large coffee and eat chocolate (or is that only me?). Self-encouragement is less about how we feel and more about what we do. Feelings are important but they can be deceptive and misleading. *Doing* is a greater sign of what we really think and believe and as we engage with purpose, it can in fact encourage us as we go.

Joseph had an excuse to give up, get bitter and get even. Sold into slavery by his brothers (he narrowly escaped death), he ends up in Egypt, far from his family but not from the presence of God. In Potiphar's house he serves so well as a slave that he gains promotion and is entrusted with the whole estate. In prison (after being accused of attempted rape) he serves so well that the warden puts him in charge of the whole prison. At one point in prison he helps a man by interpreting his dream and all Joseph asks in return is that the man, a butler to Pharaoh, remembers him. Guess what, not only did he forget Joseph, but he forgot him for two whole years.

What's the point, John? Joseph would one day become the second most powerful man in the world and a saviour of his own people as well as many others. But before he got there, he turned many trials into Mach-busting moments; each time he pressed through into excellence. One of the factors that stood out in Joseph's life is that he continued to serve wherever he was. He served his father at home, served Potiphar's household and served the prison warder. He encouraged himself and broke through the pain of disappointment by continuing to do the right thing. When the prison door did eventually open for him, Joseph only needed a shave and a change of clothes because his heart was ready! He had learned to encourage himself in the most difficult of circumstances and that had helped prepare him for the fulfilment of his destiny. Had he allowed his spirit to become bitter, the breathtaking story of Joseph would never have been told because the young dreamer would have died before he had the chance to live.

Similarly, David found strength as he encouraged himself in the Lord his God. David experienced a Mach-busting moment which transformed potential disaster into an incredible victory. David's decision ensured success for himself and for the men around him. Instead of becoming embittered he was encouraged. As we learn to encourage ourselves in the Lord we will know the thrill of success.

Notes _____

1. Raum, E., *Dietrich Bonhoeffer, Called by God* (Continuum, 2002), pp. 137–150.
2. Ibid., p. 137.
3. See Romans 4:16–25 for the full passage.

Rising Above Mediocre Expectations

On 19th August 2006, twenty-five-year-old Sam Thompson completed an amazing challenge by running fifty-one marathons in fifty days. Let me remind you that a marathon is 26 miles 385 yards long. In old money, that's really far! He began on 1st July and completed his last marathon in his home state of Mississippi ending a 1,300-mile odyssey during which time he wore out eleven pairs of running shoes. He ran a marathon in all fifty US states on consecutive days, plus an extra one in the District of Columbia, when he ran two on the same day. During each marathon he consumed 1,200 calories and then a further 5,000 after each run. He ate mainly chicken, turkey, pasta and sandwiches, boosting his calorie intake by eating lots of ice-cream and cakes. His achievement eclipsed what had been the record-breaking marathon running of Sir Ranulph Fiennes, who in 2003 completed seven marathons in seven days.

Of course, the predictions from the experts were that such a thing could not be done, that the human body would be incapable of such prolonged physical exertion, that Mr Sam Thompson from Mississippi was expecting way too much. The irony was the exact opposite. Throughout the adventure his body grew stronger and his times faster. Incredibly he ran his penultimate marathon (that's number fifty) in his best ever time of three hours and twenty-nine minutes. In the words of the man himself, "The human body is capable of doing a lot more than people give it credit for."[1]

Everybody say "Wow"! Undoubtedly, Sam's achievements are pretty exceptional, even for endurance athletes, but this running man did not allow the expectations of those around him to dictate to his dream. He researched, prepared, trained and took all sensible precautions for his success, but at the root of his achievement was the belief that it could be done, that his body was capable of taking the strain and pressing through to his personal Mach-busting moment. He refused to live in limitation and pursued high expectations.

Mediocre expectations have prevented many who have had the gifts, potential and opportunity to break through from ever doing so because they are convinced, for one reason or another, that it just cannot be done. As someone once put it, "Whether we think we can or we think we can't, we'll always be right."

What are your expectations for yourself, your family or your church? What factors are setting the boundaries of the expectations in your life? Could your expectations be described as mediocre or magnificent?

Take a moment to read 2 Kings 4:1–7.

I remember going into MacDonalds one day.

"Would you like to go large?"

I looked at the girl taking my order, not really certain how to answer that question when she spoke again.

"Would you like to go large on your meal?"

For an extra payment, I could go large on my fries and drink (and of course I did). But it was the question which caught my attention. She was giving me the choice to stay as I was or go large.

The Bible declares that God is for us, that He has a plan and future for each one of us. It declares He is committed to making us the best we can be, so that we live life as it was originally designed to be lived and touch His world with His glory. But so many times it's our limited expectations which stop God from doing in us what He wants and from performing through us what He can. God so often wants us to go large, but too often we hesitate.

In the story in 2 Kings 4, we read of a woman in desperate need. Her husband had died, leaving the family in debt with no prospect of paying the creditors. Her two sons faced the possibility of a life of slavery if the debts could not be paid. (Leviticus 25:39–40 stipulates that a debtor who could not pay his debt was obliged to serve his creditor as a slave until the year of Jubilee, which occurred every fifty years.) She turns to the prophet Elisha for help and he offers her a way out through a miracle of enlargement. God would take her little, *"Your servant has nothing . . . at all . . . except a little oil"* (v. 2), and increase it.

Elisha's words are amazing:

> *"Borrow **as many empty jars as you can** from your friends and neighbours. Then go into your house with your sons and shut the door behind you. Pour olive oil from your flask into the jars, setting each one aside when it is filled."*
>
> (2 Kings 4:3–4 NLT, emphasis added)

The key to this miracle was capacity. The prophet put no limit on the number of jars the woman could have. This was entirely her decision. She could settle for 100 or bring in 100,000. Elisha simply promised her whatever she brought, would be filled! In the midst of an incredibly challenging time for her, he was asking her to go large, to raise the level of her expectations beyond anything she had experienced before. He promised the oil would flow, as long as she had capacity to contain it. Note his encouragement to her, *"Borrow **as many** empty jars as you can"* (NLT, emphasis added), *"Don't ask for just a few"* (NIV). The prophet urged her to go large, to raise the level of her expectation, and take God at His word and so experience His supernatural provision.

What would you have done? How many jars would you have brought?

To engage in this miracle, the woman in question had to address two key challenges.

1. She had to break the mould of limitation

Try and stand in her sandals for a few minutes. This is a woman who had been accustomed to hardship. She had become used to a life of "not enough" or at best "just enough". Since her husband had died, life had been even harder and when questioned by the prophet about what she had, the only thing of value in her home was a little oil. Poverty and hardship were her way of thinking and a way of life. But now, she was being offered the chance to move beyond "not enough" and "just enough" to "more than enough". For someone who had become used to poverty and meagre scraps that was much tougher than it might sound. She was shaped in a mould of limitation, which had been forged by experience, environment, beliefs and maybe even her friends. She had come to expect little because little was the reality of her experience. The challenge facing her was that in order to get into jar-collecting mode, she had to break free from the mould of limitation and poverty that had become her way of life.

Mediocre expectations are shaped in the crucible of limitation and lack. I once heard a story of an old lady, whose home had become run down. She rarely put her heating on and lived on meagre rations of food. But when she died, it was discovered that she had thousands of pounds in the bank. One withdrawal could have changed everything, but she had been raised not to be greedy, to be prudent and go without, so the money stayed in the bank and though well-off, she lived in poverty.

Offer a box of chocolates to a child and say, "You can have as many as you like." Their eyes will light up and they'll gladly help themselves. Do the same thing to an adult, and the chances are they'll take only one or two with the response, "I must not be greedy ... that's fine for me ... two is enough!" We limit ourselves because we've been taught to by life, family, values and beliefs or by the fear that to eat the whole box will be viewed as greedy and self-indulgent. It would only be greedy and selfish if we had been offered one. It isn't greedy if we've been offered the box!

God offers His children so much and we expect and accept so little. We're conditioned by our world into thinking that taking only a little and expecting only enough is virtuous. Certainly, self-control and prudence are to be admired, but not when God is offering us unlimited resources. Limitation permits us to ask for only a few jars, but the prophet urged her to get as many as she could. These limitations cause us to think small and negative, but God wants us to think large and positive. Meagreness of heart encourages us to accept poverty and containment, when God's lavish generous heart inspires us to expect prosperity and advancement. God is not limited, but we are! He's able and willing while so often we are fearful and hesitant. So much more awaits us beyond the boundaries of limitation, but we must have the courage to address our limitations and break them.

Peter said:

> "His divine power has given us everything we need for life and godliness through our knowledge of him who called us by his own glory and goodness."

(2 Peter 1:3)

Everything we need has already been deposited in our account, but we need to understand this and learn to draw upon what has already been given to us. Limitation will prevent us from collecting the jars, or if we do, we'll only take a few. If God has lifted the limits, then why should we live under them?

2. She had to raise the bar of expectation

The limitations of our experience can often militate against the expansion of our expectations. The only limitation on this miracle was down to how many jars could be found. What if the woman had gone beyond her village looking for jars? What if she had gone regional or national? What if she had seized the awesome possibilities of this miracle and accumulated hundreds of thousands of jars? *All of them would have been filled!*

Note the words of Elisha:

> *"Go, sell the oil and pay your debts. You and your sons can live on what is left."*
>
> (2 Kings 4:7)

God was not only interested in meeting her needs, but in going beyond her needs to bless her with abundance. Had He only been focused on paying her debt, then He could have instructed her on exactly how many jars would be needed for this task. But God wanted to do more for her than just clear her debt, He wanted her to experience and live in the power of His abundance in her life. Everything over and above "need" was hers to enjoy and God wanted her to have as much of it as possible. She went expecting a few bills to be paid while God's agenda was much bigger than that. It was one of blessing.

Jesus feeds thousands of people with a packed lunch and

there are twelve baskets full to the brim left over. Why? He's the God of more than enough! At Jesus' request, Peter goes fishing after a fruitless, frustrating night and catches so many fish that he has to call his friends to help him. Why? He's the God of more than enough!

Paul declared:

> *"Now to him who is able to do immeasurably more than all we ask or imagine, according to his power that is at work within us . . . "*
>
> (Ephesians 3:20)

Imagine it . . . He's way ahead of us, immeasurably more!

Ask it . . . He has the resources, immeasurably more!

But incredibly, the power with which He does all this is already within us. We need to raise the level of our expectation of God and, in partnership with Him, of ourselves. We expect so little and hope for such small return. We content ourselves to live in the land of "just enough" and we rarely dare to ask, "Please Lord, can I have some more?"

I have no idea how many jars the woman eventually collected but I do know, that had she collected some more, God would have filled them. She realized a little late the enormity of her miracle and its awesome potential. She asked for more jars but there wasn't one left. As soon as the last jar was filled the Bible declares, *"Then the oil stopped flowing"* (2 Kings 4:6). It didn't stop flowing because God ran out of oil but because the woman ran out of jars. If only she could have found a few more . . .

The woman experienced a Mach-busting moment. She moved from poverty to prosperity by daring to break the mould of her limitation and raise the bar of her expectations. Whether she could or should have gone further and collected more jars or not, is a matter of conjecture and debate. The fact is she obeyed and gathered what she could according to the faith she had. The oil flowed and her life changed. She pushed through beyond the shakes into success.

The story is told that an explorer, while travelling through a diamond-rich African nation came across two boys playing in the dirt. As the explorer watched them he noticed that the boys were playing a game similar to marbles. They laughed, engrossed in their game and did not notice as the man approached for a closer look. What he saw amazed him. They were playing marbles with diamonds! The children had no idea of the value of the jewels they had in their hand, the wealth and riches that lay covered in the red African dust. To them they were just stones and they were content to have some fun.[2]

What limitation has been placed on your life? Maybe experience has discouraged you from expecting anything more from God than you already have? Could it be your friends have convinced you that this is your lot and you should settle for it? Perhaps your own beliefs are setting the limit for your thinking, keeping you a small person, with little ambition and no expectation that "more than enough" could be your reality. Maybe you haven't realized that the little stones in your hands are God-given diamonds. It is time to smash the limitations that stop you going forward in God and raise your level of expectation of who God is and what He can do for and through you. It is time to realize who you are and what lies within your grasp. God is for you. God has more for you and if you dare to believe it, the possibilities are beyond your wildest dreams.

Notes

1. Article from *The Times*, Wednesday, 23 August 2006, p. 31.
2. Havner, V., *Playing Marbles with Diamonds* (Baker Book House, 1985), p. 19.

CHAPTER 10

Failure Isn't Falling Down, It's Staying Down

Joe Rosenthal was the photographer who took one of the most iconic pictures in the history of the United States military endeavour. His photograph, taken on the 23rd February 1945, shows the US flag being raised by six soldiers (five Marines and one naval corpsman), on Mount Suribachi, located on the strategic Japanese island of Iwo Jima. Rosenthal, a photographer with the Associated Press caught the moment "as much by luck as by design". This image "blurred and indistinct yet unforgettable, became the most recognized, the most reproduced, in the history of photography".[1]

Incredibly, it all might have been so very different for Joe Rosenthal. When the Second World War broke out he was studying at the University of San Francisco and applied to join both the army and the navy. Both rejected him, because the 5ft 5in Rosenthal was *short-sighted*! He didn't give up in his quest to serve in the war effort and in 1943 he joined the US Maritime Service, photographing convoys in the Atlantic and off the coasts of Britain and North Africa, having also distinguished himself photographing the fighting in Guam and Peleliu. Ironically, Joe Rosenthal the short-sighted army reject, became the man who in 1/400th of a second took the most famous and celebrated war picture in the history of the world.[2] Good job he didn't give up!

Somebody once said, "Failure isn't falling down, it's staying down."

It's the easiest and most natural thing in the world to stay down when we've either failed or been rejected, or our dreams and expectations have not been realized. The Mach-busting moment occurs when we get up from the ground of failure or rejection and continue to live a successful life. It's when we refuse to allow an opinion, or a decision, or a moment in time define who and what we are for the rest of our lives. Many have decided to quit right there. A shrine of excuse and limitation gets erected around the site with a regular pilgrimage to the scene of this terrible tragedy. I suggest to you, the tragedy is not so much the failure itself, but the failure to get over the failure!

Had Roy Riggles stayed in the dressing room and not come out for the second half, no-one would have blamed him. Playing in the American football Rose Bowl College final, Roy had scored a magnificent touchdown ... at the wrong end! Coach Price tried to console Roy at half time but to no avail. As his team left to take the field Roy didn't move. Coach Price spoke to Roy once more, "The game is only half over." The next day the papers declared that Roy Riggles played the second half like a man possessed.[3]

Many choose to stay in the dressing room rather than face the jeering crowd or the reminder of past failures, but if this is our decision, a Mach-busting moment will evade our grasp and we will forever be haunted and tormented by the memory of *that* failure.

> "We cannot abandon life because of its storm. The strongest trees are not found sheltered in the safety of the forest, rather they are out in the open spaces – bent and twisted by winds of

all seasons. God provides deep roots when there are wide-spreading branches."[4]

Look with me at Acts 13:13, a verse which records a key moment in a young man's life:

> *"From Paphos, Paul and his companions sailed to Perga in Pamphylia, where John left them to return to Jerusalem."*

That seems simple enough and the following verses suggest life went on as normal. However, a few verses later in the same book, in which approximately two years have passed, two great friends fall out over this incident (see Acts 15:36–41). Barnabas (whose name means Son of Encouragement) and Paul are about to embark on their second major missions journey together, when Barney makes a suggestion, "Let's take John Mark." Paul was having none of it and completely refused the possibility of him accompanying them. But why, what was the problem?

> *"But Paul did not think it wise to take him, **because he had deserted them in Pamphylia** and had not continued with them in the work."*
>
> (Acts 15:38, emphasis added)

Dr Luke had tried to be kind to the young travelling companion of Paul and Barnabas when he suggested he had simply left to go home. The truth was, and we're not exactly sure why, John Mark did a runner, he went Absent Without Leave and even though this had happened two years previously, Paul was not prepared to give John Mark a second chance. As a result, the two great men agreed to disagree, and although there seems to be no malice at all between them, they go their separate ways, Paul taking Silas and Barnabas taking his cousin John Mark.

Luke tells us plenty about the adventures of Paul throughout the book of Acts, but nothing is said of Barnabas and John Mark ... so that's the end of the story, right? Not quite.

There are three key references about John Mark throughout the New Testament, interestingly, all written by Paul:

> *"My fellow prisoner Aristarchus sends you his greetings, as does Mark, the cousin of Barnabas. (You have received instructions about him; if he comes to you, **welcome him.**)"*
>
> (Colossians 4:10, emphasis added)

> *"Epaphras, my fellow prisoner in Christ Jesus, sends you greetings. And so do Mark, Aristarchus, Demas and Luke, **my fellow workers.**"*
>
> (Philemon 23–24, emphasis added)

> *"Only Luke is with me. Get Mark and bring him with you, **because he is helpful to me in my ministry.**"*
>
> (2 Timothy 4:11, emphasis added)

It seems John Mark wasn't such a failure after all. Paul's words, recorded in 2 Timothy are probably his last to us. The passage is intimately personal as the old warrior apostle faces his end. He's been let down, disappointed and deserted by those he thought were his friends, but the former deserter gets an outstanding mention, *"he is helpful to me in my ministry."*

John Mark had failed, but he wasn't a failure. Helped and nurtured by Barnabas, the young man recovered enough to be considered again a fellow worker of Paul. Somewhere along the line he had a Mach-busting moment, broke through the pain of failure and the humiliation of rejection and got back on track to serve again.

How can we, like John Mark, get through the barrier of failure or rejection and reach success on the other side? Here are some tips to remember and practise.

1. Failure is painful but it doesn't have to be terminal

Kenny Dalglish grew up in the shadow of Ibrox and dreamed of playing for his beloved Glasgow Rangers Football Club. As a teenager he played for Glasgow United and everybody, including Dalglish, expected Rangers to ask him for a trial. His own words sum it up:

> "...no one [at Rangers] ever asked me. I never knew why. At the time I was disappointed because the team I followed, and wanted to sign for, didn't seek me out."

For so many young footballers that would have been the end of their story, but not for Dalglish. Glasgow Celtic, arch-rivals of Rangers came calling and young Kenny duly signed. Over the next twenty plus years, Kenny Dalglish enjoyed a glittering career winning every honour in the game both in Scotland and in England. He experienced European success with Liverpool, as well as winning a staggering 102 caps for the Scottish national team.

What might have happened if Dalglish had taken rejection from Glasgow Rangers as the final act in his fledgling football career? The painful experience of failure would have become terminal.

Too many allow the pain of failure to become a terminal issue in their lives. They see it as the end when really, in the context of a whole life, it is only a moment. We are the ones who make the decision as to whether the barrier of failure becomes an impenetrable wall or temporary fence. We decide whether staying on the floor is preferred to getting up again. Failure can be terminal, but it doesn't have to be!

2. Learn from it but let it go

Abraham Lincoln is regarded by many as the saviour of the American union and nation. Divided against itself over the issue of slavery, President Lincoln rose to the fight, enduring a horrific bloody civil war to see a new nation emerge. What few realize is that his journey to the White House was littered with both personal and professional failure and tragedy. Let me illustrate:

- In 1831 he was defeated for the Illinois State Legislature.
- In 1834 he was elected to the State Legislature.
- In 1843 he was defeated for the United States Congress.
- In 1846 he was elected to the Congress.
- In 1848 he was defeated for re-election to the Congress.
- In 1855 he was defeated for the U.S. Senate.
- In 1856 he was defeated for the U.S. Vice Presidential nomination.
- In 1858 he was defeated for the U.S. Senate.
- In 1860 he became President of the United States.
- In 1863 he signed the Emancipation Proclamation and delivered the Gettysburg address.
- In 1864 he is elected to a second presidential term.[5]

Even in the face of such disappointment and failure, Lincoln concluded, "'The path was worn and slippery. My foot slipped from under me, knocking the other out of the way, but I recovered and said to myself, 'It's a slip and not a fall.'"[6]

He was a great president and a great fighter. There is enough failure and rejection in this list for a dozen lives, let alone one. I haven't mentioned his business failure or family deaths that profoundly affected him. His professional career spans both failure and victory and demonstrates that we can learn from failure but that we need to let it go. What if Lincoln had held on to the stinging memory of those Legislature or Senate defeats?

Those who have lived great lives and know what it is to push through and get to the success on the other side of the shakes also know the experience of numerous failings. They can not only show you the medals, but also the scars. They can talk with great passion about the highs, but be brutally honest about the lows. But all of them have one thing in common; when it comes to failure. They've learned from it and let it go! Do what has to be done. If you need to forgive others, then do it. If you need to forgive yourself, then do it. We cannot deny our failings, but we can learn from them and make them work on our behalf.

Did you know that God does that for you?

> *"And we know that in all things God works for the good of those who love him, who have been called according to his purpose."*
>
> (Romans 8:28)

Not everything that comes our way is good, but God has made an agreement with us that He will do everything in His awesome power, to turn the negative for our good, to manipulate the pain for our good, to transform failure into something that ultimately works to our advantage. God is willing let it go and help us learn from failure, but we must be willing to take the offer.

3. Don't fight it alone

Just like John Mark, we all need a Barney! We need someone who will continue to believe in us no-matter what, someone who will fight for us and with unabated determination, pick us up when we fall. I suspect, as soon as Barnabas got back from his first missions trip with Paul, he went looking for his young cousin. I suspect he was the one who encouraged him to take the field for the second half and that he was the one who convinced John Mark that the pain he felt was not terminal. The New Testament seems to vindicate Barnabas's decision to fight for John Mark.

When wounded and hurt by failure or rejection, the temptation is to find a nice dark room, turn on some Country and Western music and live there for a while. However, the power of isolation is so potentially destructive, that if we give in to that temptation we will find that we rarely emerge better; we normally come out bitter.

Elijah was a seasoned warrior prophet who, through the Word of the Lord had brought a nation to its knees. On Mount Carmel, he took on the prophets of the false gods and won convincingly, climaxing in fire falling from heaven. At this point, the ticker tape is being prepared for the celebration drive through ... then Jezebel, the wife of King Ahab, threatens to kill Elijah and no sooner can you say "grab that prophet" than Elijah has gone on the run, in fear for his life. He runs all the way from the north to the south of the nation and into the desert. When he reaches Beersheba, the Bible says a striking thing:

> *" . . . he left his servant there, while he himself went a day's journey into the desert."*
>
> (1 Kings 19:3–4)[7]

Why did he leave his servant? Could it have been because he didn't want anyone resisting his efforts to give up and die? Alone, Elijah was certain to win the argument.

The Bible puts it succinctly when it says:

> *"If one falls down,*
> *his friend can help him up.*

But pity the man who falls
and has no-one to help him up!"

(Ecclesiastes 4:10)

One of the reasons many people never break through the barrier of failure is because they isolate themselves from outstanding friends who can help them. The Mach-busting decision will always remain the responsibility of the person facing the challenge, but good friends, who themselves know how to get through the shakes, are not to be side-lined. Failure is not a time to run away from your friends, although that's what we all feel like doing, but instead, it's a time to run to those who truly love and support us.

"True friendship is like sound health, the value of it is seldom known until it is lost."[8]

John Mark failed. He did desert Paul and Barnabas, and exposed them to even more danger as he left them light on manpower. This could have been the end for him, but the glory of this story is that it wasn't. The experience was not terminal, he learned from it and let it go, and with the help of great friends, he pushed through and enjoyed a Mach-busting moment.

Remember, failure is not falling down, it's staying down.

As you are about to finish the final chapter of this book, I pray that some of the principles contained within its pages have inspired you to move forward with the glorious adventure of your life. Many challenges lie ahead of you, but with God's grace and power, all of them can be conquered. By embracing God's truth and living out His principles, you can become a bigger and stronger person in every way, empowered to be all you were designed to be and equipped to do all He has designed for you to do. Breakthrough isn't something that will just happen to you, rather it is something you must do. But as I've tried to illustrate in this book, life beyond the shakes is possible. Mach-busting breakthrough can be for you a glorious reality. Success awaits you beyond the shakes. Press through and possess!

> *"One who breaks open the way will go up before them;*
> *they will break through the gate and go out.*
> *Their king will pass through before them,*
> *the LORD at their head."*

(Micah 2:13)

Notes

1. Bradley, J., *Flags of Our Fathers* (Pimlico, 2000), p. 3. The author James Bradley was the son of the naval corpsman, John Bradley, one of the men captured in Rosenthal's picture.
2. Obituary of Joe Rosenthal in *The Times*, 22nd August 2006, p. 49.
3. Gilpin, op. cit., p. 24.
4. Tammy Felton, *The Christian Quotation Collection* (BCA, 1997), p. 255.
5. Woodbridge, J. (gen. ed.), *More Than Conquerors* (Candle Books), pp. 14–21.
6. www.dailycelebrations.com/082001.htm – Abraham Lincoln.
7. The whole story is 1 Kings 19:1–21.
8. Charles Caleb Colton, op.cit., in *Quotations*, p. 169.

About the Author

Dr John Andrews has been in full-time leadership since 1987. Currently he serves as the Director of Training at Mattersey Hall College and Graduate School, the official Bible College of the Assemblies of God in Great Britain. He is also presently the Senior Minister of Rotherham New Life Christian Centre in South Yorkshire, England, having taken up the post in September 1997. He is a teacher with a passion to inspire and equip the Church to make God famous in their world. As well as ministering in the UK, John travels regularly to various nations of the world seeking to invest what he has, while he can.

Born in Belfast, Northern Ireland, John is married to Dawn and together they have three children, Elaina, Simeon and Beth-Anne. A graduate of the Assemblies of God Bible College, Mattersey Hall, he holds a Masters degree in Pentecostal and Charismatic Studies from Sheffield University and a Doctorate from the University of Wales.

John's hobbies include supporting his beloved football team, Liverpool, listening to music, reading and watching great movies, his favourite movie of all time being *It's a Wonderful Life*. He loves to eat and among his favourite food groups are Chinese, Italian and chocolate!

Other books by John Andrews

Available from www.esbresources.co.uk

Truthformation

ISBN 0 9546232 0 7   £4.99

For lasting change to take place on the outside, truth-change must take place on the inside. Truth not only challenges what we think about, but how we actually think, probing the framework of our belief system which in turn dictates how we live and what we live for. This book encourages you to open up your mind and engage with truth in the confidence that truth will do the rest. As Jesus said, "You will know the truth and the truth will set you free."

Loved

ISBN 0 9546232 3 1   £6.99

Why is the God who is love the best kept secret in the universe? You would think that such a prospect would be celebrated and enjoyed in the Church, trumpeted and proclaimed to a dying world. Yet somehow, this glorious truth, this life-giving message, this world-changing power, has been among the most neglected in pulpits and in mission. The story that God is love languishes in dusty recesses under a pile of issues deemed weightier and more important. But what could be more important than the understanding that at the heart of the universe, at the core of the Church and in the engine room of mission, lies the unshakeable, immeasurable reality that God is love?

Hope
ISBN 0 9546232   £6.99

This book is a celebration of hope and a journey to hope. In it you will discover a practical step by step guide to living a life of hope. God wants you to be a person who has a belief system empowered by hope, expressing itself in hopeful dreams, actions and lifestyles. Hope-filled people impact their world with life and optimism. They defy the odds, destroy cynicism and create a culture where dreams are given every opportunity to come true.

Rest
ISBN 0 9546232 1 5   £5.99

God has given us Rest so that we may enjoy life and in turn be great adverts for His life on the earth. Too many of us are working and not resting, living and not laughing, achieving and not enjoying. But look at Jesus: He had the weight of the world on His shoulders and yet He was a man at rest, loving people, living life joyfully while still totally focused on His mission. If we learn to rest we will live and work well. If we embrace rest, we will not only make it to the destination, but we will have enjoyed the journey.

Mission is Like a Box of Chocolates
£7.99

Imagine receiving a never ending supply of chocolate. Every delight and delicacy you can think of, given as a free gift and all yours! But imagine keeping all that chocolate to yourself, gorging selfishly each day, content with the goal of self-satisfaction, while so many around you have never tasted your special chocolate even once and others don't even know it exists. This book calls those who have already received Heaven's "Chocolate" to consider sharing it with those who have never tasted it and others who don't know it exists, that our focus would move away from asking for more, to looking at ways in which we can share what we have.

Other books from New Wine Ministries

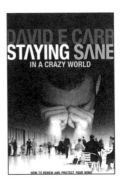

Staying Sane in a Crazy World

David Carr

ISBN 978-1-903725-42-9

£6.99

"Essential reading ... David Carr writes out of a lifetime of wrestling with the renewing and protecting of the mind with passion, clarity and conviction."

The Rt Revd Dr John Sentamu
Archbishop of York

The 5 Attributes of a Church in Revival

David Carr

ISBN 978-1-903725-65-8

£7.99

"This stunning book is a straight-talking, hard-hitting, 'Back to Basics' trumpet-call to battle-weary churches seeking revival today. David Carr speaks and writes with prophetic punch and power. I loved this book for its humorous, sharp, insightful and high-octane encouragement. It will energize receptive leaders and churches everywhere in their hot pursuit of God."

Greg Haslam
Minister, Westminster Chapel, London

Visit www.newwineministries.co.uk
for our full range of books